A Mermaid's Tears

Poetry, Prose, and Messages
for Twin Flames
and Other Soul Connections

Linda Harris

Dedication

This book is dedicated to Muse, without whom the poetry would not exist, nor would my nine-year trial by fire and then by water. It took so long only because I had that much resistance to being loved. I can't express the gratitude I feel for bringing me to a deep realization and the experience of God as Love. I AM Love. When I reached for you, I was reaching for the Divine Masculine aspect of Myself, which I saw so very clearly in you. I wish you unending happiness.

Contents

Preface

No matter who we look to for inspiration, reality is subjective. We each have our own image of a muse. If we would submit to the siren call, we could take the chance and write the music, the poem, the novel, paint the picture or sculpt that image. We could liberate ourselves from the fear of others' opinions. If we could submit to our creative streak and not worry how it's going to sound or appear to others, we could express the art within us. If we could each pay homage to our own source of inspiration, hear the song in our own hearts, learn it and sing along, we could make the world a more beautiful, more accepting place.

Nine years ago, I started this journey of self-discovery and evolution. Not the first journey I've taken, but since life is like an onion, you just keep peeling layer after layer. However, this most current journey was the first involving this soul connection and 5D stuff (getting deeper). Last night, I was reviewing this manuscript and thought I'd add a quote by Carl Jung on dreaming and the unconscious. I found several good quotes, but also found something from Joseph Campbell. It referenced The Hero's Journey, which I had studied a couple of decades ago. What caught my eye was the list of steps in the journey. As I lightly scanned it, I had to stop. Don't you love those revelations that hit you like lightning? Especially when it's so obvious you suddenly feel stupid. After all the self-discovery, all those years ago, I feel I must have forgotten how to live the epic life and settled back into a peaceful mediocrity without realizing.

Of course, when you set yourself up with the 'pre-incarnational' plan, your 'next-life syllabus', you make sure you set your alarm to wake you at periodic intervals. These are shake-up moments that pull you, by the hair if need be, into an awareness you are off track and need to get back on track. It's like a unit test and a percentage of your grade. If you aren't up to speed, you must then tackle extra credit. I feel like this is what happened. My extra credit took a long time because I forgot that nothing is impossible, and I alone have the power to choose my level of happiness, just as I alone have the power to put myself through hell.

I have to go back and study the hero's journey from a different angle this time. I must have thought, "Let's make it challenging and throw in some past-life stuff because we need to expand the 'big picture'. Add a big shot of impossibility and an intensive review of self-judgment because we haven't gotten past that yet. Oh, and motivation. Don't forget we need impetus to stick with it through the 'I'm losing my mind' phase. That should wake up anybody."

A brief summary, from my perspective, of the Divine Masculine and Divine Feminine talked about in so many twin flame groups: At the end of these nine years, these archetypes come full circle, back to Anima and Animus. Think of Animus as the inner masculine side of a woman. Carl Jung, at times, referred to the Animus as the woman's soul, but in many cases, he refers to it as the woman's unconscious. On the other hand, the Anima firmly functions as the man's soul. It is both a personal complex and an archetypal image. One that gets him in touch with his feelings and his creativity. I like to think 'muse'.

Let me wrap this up. The Animus has four stages, but that's TMI and I'm not going there, except to say: this journey, for me, evolved my Animus through stage 3 and onto 4, transcending the ordinary and mundane. My Animus, my Divine Masculine, is now a symbol for me of inner union with Divinity, reaching the point of the alchemical marriage, the inner union of duality within myself. It's fire and water, converting lead into gold. It's unconditional love, truth, and pure joy. I feel that I approached it, fell back, and approached it a thousand times before I realized I was there for the most part. It wasn't one defining moment, but a series of moments continually redefining myself. It was like rolling over in bed, knowing you are awake but drowsy and have not yet opened your eyes. Trying to stay in the memory of the dream but knowing you need to get up now.

So, before I submit my manuscript, here I am doing a huge last-minute rewrite. What had been a story about animal totems and how they represented phases of my journey, is now coming full circle to the hero's journey. Once again, this is just another layer of that blasted onion. You may think these are all separate lessons, but I'm reminded today they are all different chapters in the same damn textbook. Love, I'm here for that. Perhaps dragonflies for the power of light, peacocks for showing my true colors, mermaids for the emotional deep dive into the abyss and the phoenix for rising up and taking flight needs a place of its own (Part 1).

September 5, 2022

> *We have only to follow the thread of the hero path, and where we had thought to find an abomination, a monster, we shall find a god. And where we had thought to slay another, we shall slay ourselves. Where we had thought to travel outward, we will come to the center of our own existence. -Joseph Campbell*

A Mermaid's Tears

Part 1: A personal letter to you

Hello! Hey, I'm the super casual type so let's just have this personal talk, shall we? I'll be talking, but feel free to voice your comments audibly as we go along.

Since the last-minute rewrite, I've added this personal letter, I thought I'd move this from the preface and make it a letter to you. It's our chance to get better acquainted. Whatever you think of my poetic skill level doesn't matter. I didn't write them as a literary practice. I have shown my soul, bared my heart, in these three volumes of poetry. These are fragments of my journey. It's me painting a picture with words for myself so I can look at it. It's my own version of art. If you can feel them, then I am speaking to you. If you can't feel them, we are not only not on the same page, we probably aren't in the same metaphorical book. No problem. I did this because it's part of my journey. I did it because I must.

Consider me crazy if you will, but I want to remind you - the only opinion you need to pay attention to is your own. To quote a book I read a very long time ago, "What you think of me is none of my business." What others think of you, or anyone, is not wholly accurate. The only opinion of value comes from the person closest to you who knows you inside out. That's you.

> *Be mindful of your self-talk. It is a conversation with the universe. -Angie Karan*

Even I need to be reminded of this quote.

Previously, I had twenty years of experience as a group leader. High priestess may sound pretentious to you. However, I am not ego driven at all, so it's group leader. Before you start reading poetry, I want to interject a bit about animal totems. Why? I feel it's somewhat relevant. I taught an Animal Totem class for my students, private groups, and a few times at a local community college. More importantly, my journey animals bring energy, set tones, themes, and lessons for me, which will be most obvious in the mermaid poems.

Maybe you already know all this, but for those who do not... What is an animal totem? To put it simply, it's an animal energy that is helpful and it is a spiritual presence. That energy or spirit is walking with you as you go through life to lend its energetic expertise. This is either for a phase of growth, or a lesson you are learning. In a way, you can view them as guardians or a type of guardian angel. For the magical among us, call it a power animal or one of a number of different kinds of spirit guide. I laugh now, thinking about how the word 'patronus' came up recently.

Life totems: We have one life totem. They come in with you at birth because their energy represents your life's theme. Others may walk (swim or fly) with you over extended periods, these are journey totems. There are different levels of involvement when it comes to temporary totems. Of lesser importance overall, are animals who may only be with you a short while involving a lesson, and finally those critters who come once, or perhaps a series of times, to show you something you need to acknowledge. Some totems may be considered mythical creatures like dragons or unicorns, but maybe we can suspend judgment and stretch beyond our habitual thinking, to acknowledge this 3D reality isn't all there is. These "imaginary" creatures inhabit etheric energy realms where we can connect with them. We simply believe they don't exist because they are not within the range human eyes can see.

During this long journey, mermaids have cropped up in my writing. Not a lot at first, but I have felt the pull of the ocean ever increasingly. It's a pretty loud calling to hear the ocean from the Midwest. It is well over 1.000 miles in either direction. The deeper I got into my 'Self' for healing and understanding, the more mermaid presented itself.

Dragonfly arrived several years before. The energy was strong enough that I got a dragonfly bracelet tattoo. Both dragonfly and mermaid are aquatic (emotional) creatures, however once a dragonfly develops they leave the water and fly. These iridescent creatures inhabit two realms. With this journey totem, I have found that I too, can inhabit more than one realm. Dragonfly represents many things, most importantly transformation and the power of light. They are recognized as messengers who always find the positive, regardless how dark it seems. They also represent illusion, and the ability to see through it, a suggestion to look deeper. Dragonfly helps to adapt to rapidly changing situations. In Japan the dragonfly symbolizes victory and the courage to fly straight, overcome any obstacle. It brings a "don't look back and don't back down" message. I believe that Dragonfly is connected to this journey and my writing since they are not only water but air symbols.

Peacock showed up about three years ago, to urge me to show my true colors. Cyndi Lauper's song "True Colors" comes to mind. Phoenix, yet another transformation symbol, has recently arrived. I should say it came back again, showing me another form it takes. In addition to the western version of the phoenix there is the Chinese feng huang bird, also called the blue phoenix. If you are interested in the Chinese version of the phoenix you can research the legend. The most important thing to me about the feng huang bird is that over time, the mythology of the female gradually merged with and absorbed the male counterpart. If you are not aware, in a twin flame relationship, once the counterparts meet there is an energy dynamic that happens. There is higher-self energetic exchange, and each person leaves with some energy of the other attached. I call this a 'companion' and for those who can see and read auras, the companion is visible as an image of your counterpart, in your energy field.

Being a neurodivergent type of thinker, what comes to my mind is the Tao symbol. You have some [energetic] part of the other person, the goal is to incorporate it within. This is a form of union. You need not have a physical union, nor in many cases was it the plan. That's why separation exists, so you will do your own work. Your counterpart was meant to trigger you, awaken you to the next level in your ascension process. It certainly works! What gets your attention more than the most extreme and intense love you ever felt? Since the feng huang/phoenix came, I'm relieved to acknowledge I'm achieving some measure of inner union. I need to continue my growth by rising up now and taking to the air. Air is an element of communication, hence publishing my 'art' and here we are.

Back to mermaids. As I tried to keep afloat in the emotion ocean, mermaid showed me how to take the deep dive and do it alone. Mermaids are shy, secretive and can keep things from becoming common knowledge. She represents the ability to guard privacy and the importance of balancing one's heart and head. They are fiercely independent and nonconformist individuals. I've heard them called 'angels of the sea'. They usually appear at dawn or dusk, the "in between" times (those times are so magical). It's also said they only show themselves to those having a pure heart. Some legends state that when Mermaids weep, each falling tear turns into a pearl.

I read an interesting tidbit somewhere that Mermaids originate from Atlantis, having been shapeshifters. Following Atlantis' demise, they moved to the etheric realm and we can connect with them there. As etheric beings, they have no boundaries concerning time and its perceived constraints. Mermaids can teach you to walk through different worlds. Mermaid is feminine energy, she has wisdom and is as insightful as she is playful. She too, represents transformation and dwells in more than one realm. Her transformation is between sea and land, but always maintaining her freedom, sensuality and magic. Finally, mermaid guides us to remain true to who we are. So keep it real. Be your authentic self because true colors really are beautiful.

So, welcome to my world. In this volume, I finally have enough courage to let it all hang out. If you want to know my heart, just read. These are actual journal entries from the last nine years, excerpts from sent and unsent letters to my muse, and notes to myself. He has seen most of the contents in these three volumes of poetry plus some not included here. Still, there is new poetry for him to discover in these pages as well. As fantastic and absurd as it sounds, this is not fiction. Please note, I am not making any claims on his experience. I am reporting only my experience, my perception, understanding and interpretation of my experience. I can tell only my story, not his. His side is none of my business, but

I've always told him straight-up how I see it.

It's been an interesting life, though many would call it hard or unfortunate. Hard maybe, but not unfortunate. It was all character building. I am so blessed. It's my opinion that counts here and I'm sticking with it being an interesting life. I like to say life is a roller coaster, sometimes a bungee jump, but always an adventure. Once you get past polio, scoliosis, being abused, neglected and abandoned as a child, surviving domestic violence that nearly killed me, and then breast cancer, it would seem everything else is easier. Umm, no. The struggle to learn to love myself unconditionally, and to accept and embody unconditional love was my hardest battle. I am not a human with spiritual experiences. I am a soul, a stream of consciousness, having human experiences.

Lion's Gate August 8, 2022

Part 2: Poetry and Prose -
Selections From 2013-2022

1

In reflections at the water's edge, as time starts rolling backward,
clouds appear to move upstream, white paper gliders on the water.
Far across the ocean, love piles up in great waves on your shore.

2 Putting the books into perspective

The Peach Blossoms experiment, I needed to be brave.
Testing unknown waters instead of simply jumping in.
With Wine and Roses, I found it was harder to behave
but I am very clear that loving you is not a sin.
Not some lunatic, nor am I deluded or debased,
there's a bigger picture here, and I'm certainly tuned in.
I see past what eyes can look at, beyond what bodies chase.
I took the dive in Mermaid's Tears - a deep sea tailspin.

A book to send my poetry, how else could I let you know?
I had to share new verses, our communication's been
sort of touch and go. Left with dreams, the path to heaven
that they show.
We never are alone; I'm at your side. You are here, within.
We can sail the galaxy, run on the beach, or fly away.
Everything will be alright. I'm doing well, as you will see.
Unseen but ever present, my devoted heart will stay
because... you are always who you are, and I am always me.

3

That summer afternoon alone, I slowly climbed the hill.
You waited there for me that day, our one wish to fulfill.
You lay me down, in afternoon's most glowing vibrant hours,
our witnesses the sun and sky, a field of wildflowers.
We whiled away the hours, I frayed my fragile gown.
If your kisses were the ocean then I would gladly drown.
You never said you loved me, but I knew both touch and gaze.
I wish, once again, we'd make more transcendental days.

4

(Note: The between times are Mermaid times, borrowed time,
stolen moments.)

Those sweet, delicious moments between sleeping and awake
are spent in reverie. The bliss is more than I can bear.
A sacred time and place - between. So joyful my heart aches,
and every time my dream allows, my thankfulness a prayer.
Spooning in the morning sweetly, please tell me that you
know.
I doubt that this is heaven, the arousal too intense,
and still my love for you is pure and bright as driven snow.
My heart pours out devotion, and my darling, it's immense.
Spooning in the morning, I can feel your body's heat.
It's warm and tantalizing, it's delightful and sublime.
Snuggled close behind me, I feel your precious heartbeat,
thrill at the sound... and love you 'in between' on borrowed
time.

5

People simply laugh behind me, perhaps they roll their eyes,
they cannot believe, it's outlandish, too odd and bizarre.
How can you tell if one's soul deeply loves another soul?
They do not understand and think it's probably all lies—
that I'm addled, delusional, confused, and there you are!
They say it is my fantasy. I'm mental, it's an imaginary role.
But I've always been observant and I am the outside one,
I think and feel differently than most (to say the least)
from your common, everyday, ordinary sort of muggle.
I have my own unique path, my own private race to run.
Seems my taste for eccentricity has not decreased.
This path is brutal, but I can't quit because I struggle.

6

Those long walks along the beach,
you within my nightly reach,
savoring sweet salty kisses
when we made our starfish wishes.
Barefoot, running here and there,
soft wind blowing through our hair.
Oh, if I could travel time,
I'd bring back the days that you were mine.
The nights, so warm in your embrace,
reaching out, I held your face,
the galaxy our sky above.
When we were so deep in love
I dreamed in shades of mermaid scales
and iridescent peacock tails,
of pearlescent dragonflies
and brightly banded sunset skies.
Dreams as golden as the sand
when you and I walked hand in hand.
These precious memories I keep
...as long as I can stay asleep.

7

When the bliss can carry me
for hours on end in ecstasy,
I gave up long ago, asking why.
Liquid love seeps out my eye
and trickles slowly down my face,
Beloved, eons can't erase
the love I've carried all this time.
Love which all the universe
could not extinguish nor could confine.

8

It was a windy day, that day we picnicked at the beach,
laughter, squeals of joy, your 'em-ocean' mermaid within
reach.
A day the sun shone brightly, the breeze ruffling our hair -
I think it's accurate to say, the day was more than fair.
As though a dream became alive, you thought that you would
run
down to the beach to fly a kite - shouting it would be fun.
The memory of that red kite stays with me yet today.
That red kite and you, sometimes, feel so very far away.

9

The sunlit day, on the beach, flying that red kite
nothing I have known before, or since, has felt so right
except those moments gazing deeply in your eyes.
That's when I am home in our private paradise.
But nothing known on earth could have prepared me for
the day that you said you would be walking out the door.
Yet two days later, here you are, back in my life again.
How odd is this existence, how strange time is, and then
how convoluted things appear in this reality,
when soul to soul I love you, to the nth degree.
How can I explain it, when most people don't believe?
It's only an illusion that you've left me here to grieve.
Yet you come to me and warmly smile, deep into the night
and I'm back on the beach with you, flying that red kite.

10

When I see you, the rhythm of my heart quickens,
each beat a hymn of devotion. Every tear a serenade,
a rhapsody for you. Each soft and salty drop contains
a sea of infinite love for you... and I have cried oceans.

11

Your smile made my heart melt, in the midst of winter snow.
The frozen heart that I had closed, with nothing left to show
until the day that you brought spring and sunshine to my
door.
Flowers bloomed and ocean waves left kisses on the shore.
I felt the breeze, a warm caress, looked to a clear blue sky.
I know you'll never look my way, I don't need to ask why -
Though love's flame is blazing hot, the soul itself has grown.
For even flowers bow to fates, when seeds of love are sown.

12

Each night I lay awake and wait for sleep,
and every night I seek for you, it seems.
If only you could find me in your deep
and darkly shrouded dreams.
Together we could visit all the stars,
numinous and mystical realities.
The universe, my darling, would be ours
to dance through loosed from our mortality.
Where we go when we are sleeping,
I cannot say. But perhaps that place redeems
our deepest wish. Then, in your safekeeping,
I could be the woman with you in your dreams.

13

I cannot tell your sorrows by looking at your face.
Your worries and disappointments do not show.
However, in your eyes, the burden leaves its trace,
and comfort for your heart I would bestow.
Solace, and the love I nurture in a deeply tender space
if only I were at your side. If only you could know
my love is not a love that time and distance can erase.

14

What would the rest of my life be without you?
Alone, wandering the beach, searching high and low
looking for someone who knows me through and through.
Seeking for my muse who will inspire, bring the flow
and sweet bliss bestow upon this humble heart.
I wouldn't want to know what life was like alone
again, without your presence - I'd lose my art.
If only you keep shining, I can hold my own.

15 ...tiny shiny dreams

Longing sticks in my heart, like taffy in my teeth today.
I think of you and your dear, sweet presence.
It's yet another piece of candy, but it's my delight.
What can I do with this unchanging heart? It's in the way.
There's nothing I can change, or say in my defense
because every time I see you, the flames inside ignite.
I'll put them in a box on the top shelf, my shiny dreams.
On occasion take them out, for affectionate review.
In your absence I will love you; after all, it is my choice.
You may think that I have gone to ridiculous extremes
but you haven't got a clue what it means... that I love you.
I write poems, simply because I have no other voice!
Though my arms are empty now, my heart's still full of you
and I will hold on tightly - to these, my tiny, shiny dreams.
Because I cannot bring myself to stop, no matter how
deceiving.
After plunging in those depths inside your eyes, I always knew
I must endure. I'll carry on, my fragmented hopes still gleam.
I will never give up hope, and I will never stop believing!

16

The Sakura are blooming! From the past,
a memory crashes in like breaking waves,
and the image confronts my present.
I watch an ocean of cherry blossoms
scatter petals in the wind like sea spray.
How lovely you looked, shining in the sun.
The tawny-skinned, mahogany-eyed god
in my eyes was you. That unforgettable smile,
I can't erase you or that memory from my mind.
It's mine forever. Even if that April was centuries ago.

17

I die a little death, much like that of sleep
and the heart pumps out a love too deep to keep -
so I bleed salt water tears, imagine my worst fears
though they are all illusion, all distorted smoke and mirrors.
How you look, your eyes, and your soul lit up like stars
show me I am captive, without any chains or bars.

18

You never have to ever wonder why.
I am constant, and from your side, I vow I will not stray.
Above all, this love I have, I could not - would not deny.
Not to anyone, anywhere, any 'when', in any way.
If they ask, I'd have to answer, you give me wings to fly,
admitting I'm enchanted and entranced without delay.
Each day I fall in love with you once more, but Eros' dart
has pierced me so often, I bear stigmata of the heart.

19

Today I complained about the rain,
forgetting it's these gray days that I feel you best.
It's those stormy nights when you ease the pain
of your absence and I finally get some rest.

Today I complained, but that won't happen again.

I am thankful for clouds and thunder,
for every shower and downpour.
I bless and thank the skies I'm under.
I dearly love the rain, but love you more.

20 Thoughts

Each thought carries an ocean of hope, despair, joy and grief.
When sending you my love, those thoughts, mere sighs
and companions of the heart whose life is all too brief -
They are but shooting stars... as they burn across the skies.

21

How simple and sweet the thought,
I love you... You don't have to do anything.
You don't have to be anything, or be anywhere.
You just have to be, and in your being
I will cherish you, and pour this unending love
into all your deepest places. I will fill you,
and when your heart overflows, perhaps
some of that love will spill in my direction.
If it does not, I won't hesitate a moment,
and I'll continue to send my thriving adoration
until there is a large and constant heap at your feet -
so you may walk in love, all your days.

22

Thank you for our rendezvous,
our secret place upon the hill,
for windy walks on the empty beach,
the times we sit together being still.
For all the times you held me
and chased me laughing through the field,
thanks for every single moment shared.
Because of you, my heart has healed.

23

In loving you I grasp the rose, exquisite is the scent,
inhaling fragrance that I swear is truly heaven-sent.
The velvet petals like your lips, promising delight.
That ruby rose I unyieldingly grasp so tight
is my solace and my joy, even though I often bleed.
While rose-red blood drips from the thorns, my heart sighs in
its greed.

24

As long as the moon graces the night sky,
for as long as the sun continues to burn
my heart will never waver, or be shy.
I will love you boldly through every twist and turn,
that fate may throw in the path ahead.
As long as stars continue brightly shining,
I'll find my way to you. I'll not be misled
nor distracted by those fools, true love declining,
for an erotic moment here and there.
I can stay the course and I'll live alone
until the day comes, when without a care
we find within each other our forever home.

25 resurrection/reincarnation

If one day it gently rains, and a fragrant breeze is warm,
should you suddenly have thoughts of me
as if that breeze was whispering my name,
and telling you that I have gone to be reborn.
I'll be waiting on our hilltop, standing by the tree
hoping I can see you, my heart still vividly aflame.
But should you have yet, a great long time to live,
may that rain gently wash away all recollection
so you'll have a whole heart that you can fully give.
Go find your happiness, I am content in my reflection.
Samadhi bound, I overcome the earthly need for you
yet I'm sure it will revive in time for my next resurrection.

26

Waiting, I'm a pebble in the river.
Water flows around, life passes by.
The river flows, it covers and surrounds.
Water, like love, refines and wears me down
and without the slightest quiet sound,
my edges become smooth and round, and
someday, I'll be a grain of sand - still waiting.

27

I call to you in a secret language
from our secret world.
Rise and fly with me to that place
where there is only love
and truth and light.
In that golden field
or on the flowered hilltop
we will shine like two suns.
Knowing all there is...
is love.

28

I can count the ways I love you and the reasons why.
I could list all of your great attributes and talents.
It would be quite a list and there's still much I don't know.
But what I do know is simple and profound, it's this -
when I fall into your eyes, the world fades away.
Nothing else exists but you and I, and I don't care.
There is no time but now, that I'm aware.
There is no place, there's only space, but no despair
because you and I are the universe, dancing with itself.

29

Yes, I am the candle, you the luminous, radiant flame
whose purpose is to warm my life and heal the past's deep
pain.
Without you, I've no purpose, I cannot pierce the night;
a candle without flame is useless, I cannot shine my light.
I am the wick, and you, the spark, the reason I exist.
For what good is a candle, if the flame's what I resist?
So use me up, consume me, our passion burning bright;
let's spend what time we're given, in luminous delight.

30

Note: In a hard life, sometimes you don't care if you keep
breathing, until someone smiles

.

The special gifts you give me,
the things that bring me energy.
They feel like dappled morning sunlight,
a vast expanse of stars at night,
a warm and scented breeze in spring.
In these, I find the strength you bring.
Without knowing of these treasures
you have blessed me beyond measure.
All you have to do is smile...
and simply breathing is worthwhile.

31

Those few times, suns exploded, stars were born,
meteors pulled into orbit, and galaxies were formed.
Heart expanded while my mind was blown.
Would I have done this had I known?
As my body liquefied, I could only mutely cry
it's too exquisite... finding heaven in your eyes.

32

Happy without measure. How can it be thus?
When joy cascades, it overflows, because we are an 'us'.
Never doubt I love you, and eternally means still.
There never was a time I didn't, and I will until
the sun burns out, and the universe no more exists.
I will not, cannot forget you. My heart and soul insist.

33

The day you walked into my life,
my heart was no longer my own.
That day was the start of a journey
into the depths of my soul only to find
it too, was not mine alone.
Little did I know when I fell in love with you,
I would fall in love with myself and the world.
The limits of my longing would stretch out to the stars
and I'd reach for you, in a way beyond imagination.
Beyond a tangible reality, to find we really are
forever linked - and being separate isn't real.
I can touch you across an ocean vast,
not move a single inch... and feel you.

34

Your sensual fingertips are leaving light trails in the dark,
phosphorescent tracers, rising slowly off my skin.
I feel this longer than you've lingered. You've left your mark.
Watching in wonder, the light trails fade, vaporous and thin.
What kind of comfort is this? There's such beauty in the light!
You can't comprehend, it doesn't matter. Even I don't understand
this phantom lover, who comes softly to me in the night.
I know it's you, having time and distance spanned.

35

I do not wish to hold your body.
I wish to hold your heart, and
your spirit - I've embraced it from the start.
I do not wish to live with you but oddly
I'm walking at your side and daily I expand
while loving from a distance, heart to heart.
While it may seem we don't match, I embody
a soul in love with yours and blazing I withstand
the scorching heat of passion while I impart
this one love for my only, from the start.

36

A starfish, not moving, I'm dying on the beach.
Out of kindness, you plucked me from the sand
and returned me to the ocean, far from your reach.
I die a different death without you. Understand,
I cannot tell you this - for I am without speech,
my happiness was found within my hero's hand.

37 Alternate Starfish

You must know you're my hero, I'm the starfish on the beach.
I was barely living when you plucked me from the sand.
Life returned to me but you were gone, and I cannot reach
to tell you that you changed me, inside out, please
understand.
I sent you some poetry, my undying love in each,
because you woke my fading heart, I found joy in your hand.
Just know this heart is yours alone... forever and a day.

38

Love is that warm light place to which we all return,
or want to, that eternal source from whence we came.
Oft times this life is far too cold for a gentle fern
and we desire to sleep entwined within our love's embrace.
Too soon great longing overcomes, and makes the passion
burn
inside the breast, without a rest, its beating to discern.
How came I here, to this warm, light place so late in life?
Why was it you who woke me? I have yet to learn,
but I'll forever cherish blessings heaped upon
this solitary soul. You see, it's only heart that yearns.
So from afar, I wait... as season after season turns.
I swear I'll love you only - til the heavens are adjourned.

39

The scented pearly petals at pre-dawn's first rosy blush,
or crimson sunset, purple dusk, and silver moonlight's hush,
these entrancing moments etched and suspended in my mind.
And more, deemed divinely and so exquisitely designed.
Yet none compare to his bright eyes - stars shining in the
deep.
None as enchanting as my love, when I watch while he sleeps.

40

For you, I will be as a great tree with deep roots,
shelter you in storms and give up the sweetest fruits.
In autumn I will wear a brightly, multi-colored gown
and drop my leaves as coverlets for you when you lie down.
I will be constant in my love. Rooted there, I'll never leave.
Sleeping in the winter I'll dream of spring, and I'll believe
you'll come to see me blooming. I'll shed my fragrant flowers
one by one, to perfume for you these idle happy hours.
As you rest beneath my boughs, I will listen to your song.
Come to me, know I am waiting. I have been waiting long.

41

Waking up this morning, your touch tender and light
but in the dark it's tinder for the fire in the night.
Gazing in your eyes the heat of love ignites a flame.
I linger there, and I would dare to say no one's to blame.
for the ancient war that's playing out. And on a flowered
hilltop
we meet, embrace, all reason flung aside, find we cannot stop.
Your body bears the remnant marks of every wound you have.
The heart equally cut and bruised, in need of healing salve.
Your battle scars, reminding me, we must love when we can.
I hold Beloved close to me... his life didn't go as planned.
Waking up this morning, I deeply feel the gratitude.
The warmth of you so close incites a sexy attitude.
Aroused, I go limp at words like thrust and pierce -
I clearly see the warrior, and though gentle, he is fierce.

42

I believe in Karma, I know it's real and true.
In knowing everything sent out will return to you
I am mesmerized in shining light and nimbus hue—
it showers over me. I recognize anew...
it is the life, and all the love that I had sent to you.

43

That look you get when you silently gaze off into space,
it's a blank expression, but closer study of your face
and I see a touch of whimsy, perhaps a secret dream.
You are completely lost in thought, you're far away it seems.
I wish with everything I am, that I could see inside
I'm here for you if ever there are things you would confide,
but then you'd lose that mystery... or maybe not.
I won't invade the only truly private space you've got.
Perhaps this pensive mood that I interpret as remote
is nothing more than reading or you're looking for a quote.

44

I don't love lightly. I may fall in quickly,
I may have even fallen in by accident
but I am in completely until the end.

45

I'm getting used to the ebb and flow,
the ins and outs and round-abouts,
the up and down, the come and go.
Always I return without an end.
I see within the picture, you and I
weaving threads in the tapestry of life.
One who's full of youth, one waits to die.
The crossing of the threads, both joy and strife.
I know only this, in the poetry I send
I'm always with you at the last,
for in the end, the love always transcends.

46

I must have told myself a thousand lies.
It would be easy to say some short and sweet goodbyes,
that I could get over you, it simply is a choice
But then I hear you whispering in that sultry voice
and I forget all cause to go, and fall in love again.
Love written, not on clouds, but on paper with a pen.

I can hear you when you whisper, it's your heart that speaks.
Somewhere beyond the blue, a clouded, shrouded memory
leaks.
I love you far too much to let you walk away.
I'll fight for you, even though it's me I fight today.
Happiness has filled my heart; I don't recall since when.
For you I will forget past pain, and fall in love again.

47

How sweet to think your heart could love my heart.
That's all. No more. I don't need your body next to me,
you don't need to show you care. There isn't anything to start.
Nothing there to end, just love, deep and full, wide as a sea.
No expectations, no opinions. Only you and me, taking part
in this lovely thought. Oh how I wish you could agree,
to a love affair - unlike any other, just heart to heart.
No more... except, our souls will merge to some degree.
There won't be any reason I could think of to depart.
There's no status or appearance for concern, none you can see.
This is simply sharing a sweet thought... and loving heart to
heart.

34

Part 3: Whispers and Sighs and All the Deep Dives

It is by going down into the abyss that we recover the treasures of life. Where you stumble, there lies your treasure. -Joseph Campbell

OMG I have stumbled! Over and over. I feel so slow-witted, yet I'm not slow. I'm analytical and thorough. I'm self-checking, self-responsible and extremely curious. All this before realizing how it compared to the hero's journey. About soul connections - I wanted to understand how it works, under what laws does this sort of [weird] thing operate? What are the rules? Can I make it stop if I want to stop? How can I learn the energetic 'mechanics' of this? What if this, or what if that? Are there stages or phases? Dark nights of the soul, which I've seen abbreviated as "dnots", is one of those phases. There isn't just one. You can have a series of these existential crises as you peel off the layers of false beliefs and ego on your way to authenticity and Unconditional Love (recognizing your inherent divinity).

The journey is a long, strange and winding road, all of it uphill (think ascension) except for the recurring plunges into the abyss where we spend our dnots. It's that seemingly bottomless chasm, that dark place we have tossed our trash. The abyss is littered with crushed dreams, broken promises, scraps of dying hope and all the things that broke our hearts or hurt us in any way. It's the subconscious file drawer for the parts of ourselves we reject or fear. It's our storage for pain, fear, and despair, called our shadow. When we want to move on, we often just toss the remnants into the abyss without a proper resolution. Now you need to go back and clean it all up. When you do, there you find your treasure. You find joy. The prize the hero has originally sought becomes secondary. The personal transformation experienced is now the prize, the new liberation of the heart and mind.

In this soul connection I experience, such as it is, I had felt like Alice falling down the rabbit hole. Falling for hours at a time. On occasion, I spent days descending in a fall. During those times I didn't - and couldn't think about having a Light or the need to turn it on. I just felt the feelings and wrote them. This was part of my process. Those moments of despair, which were then followed by a breakthrough. Also repeated over and over for these last 3,248 days, and well over 3,500 attempts at poetry. I'm a transmuter. I wade into my pain, sink to the bottom, explore the limits of it and then wait. That's why I'm good at waiting. When it becomes still, when there is no more resistance, the Light comes on. As the Light grows, I rise and come out of it. Until the next trip down the rabbit hole. I can so relate to parts of the Matrix movie.

A major obstacle confronts the hero, and the future begins to look dim: a trap, a mental imprisonment, or imminent defeat on the battlefield. It seems like the adventure will come to a sad conclusion, as all hope appears lost. But hope remains and it is in these moments of despair when the hero must access a hidden part of himself

Nights through dreams tell the myths forgotten by the day. -Carl Jung

48

Sunning on the golden shore, waiting by an azure sea.
Seasons pass by faster now, I'm in slow motion as I sigh.
How can time speed up so quickly? It seems to fly by me.
How can the world fade away? It seems, all reason to defy
what is known, what's possible and to what degree.
I slip back in the ocean, these many years have passed
and this solitary mermaid's heart still remains the same.
It holds within a depth of love in this life unsurpassed,
and my mantra whispered day and night, it is his name.
The love I gave, refused, so this love will be my last.
This unseen, lonely lover, will be waiting in the deep
for dreams to come and rock me gently, peacefully to sleep.

49

You woke up something in me, thereby
it will not go back to sleep.
It won't go away, and it won't die -
though I have buried it quite deep.

This fire has no end, no start.
Your inner self, no castle but a keep.
Unable to obtain your heart,
this fate is shallow, love is deep.

The river flows like liquid fire
and what I'm feeling won't abate.
Perhaps I will not quench desire,
but will sit silently and wait.

50

I cannot cut you off and don't know what else to do
since my entire being is occupied by you.
I held you softly in my heart, what happened I can't say
but I drew you close and held you tighter by the day.
Perhaps it was my heart that sighed a quiet need.
It grew itself some longing, and then a hungry greed.
It started to consume me and left me feeling down.
The joy that flooded in became a sea in which to drown.
I'm faced with this dilemma and must now make a choice
to create some space between us, yet allowing love its voice.
To quell this adoration that over-spills my human form
is death by deprivation. What rites must I perform?
I don't know how to do this! I can't just let you go.
What do I do with all the love? Where do I let it flow?
What do I do with all the love, as it immortal grows?

51

Even standing next to you, if I handed you my heart
you would not take it, nor would you look my way.
I'd stand there bleeding, no will to turn away and then depart.
Yet, next to you, there in the blinding brightness of day
I'd think of things I want to say, and mentally pursue my art
and compose a poem in my mind. That heart... it is still
beating.
But I'd take my poem and your name, and etch them on this
heart
if it would please you. Perhaps one day, for a moment fleeting
you might notice this heart had dimmed - but with your gaze,
restart
and blaze again! The embers of this love would reignite.
I'd feel again the things I crave to feel, and resurrect the part
that faded there, without your care, and once more shine its
light.

52

I grieve for the lack of you, and this
vacant space where you had made your home.
I think of your scent and I recall the bliss it brought.
How many hours spent in your eyes? I sought
my comfort there, my peace and rapture too.
No counting all the tears, or the blood it drew
when I tore myself apart. Was it to pull you out
...or to try in vain to find you there?
I fell in love with every single wound and scar.
It's your heart and mind, and everything you are.
Now, looking out a clouded pane of glass askew,
a window I can't open, nor can I reach through.
I recognize I'm up against a wall I cannot breach
You fade from view. I finally accept you're out of reach.

53

I thought the aching was all over, yet I feel it here.
Pulling me beneath the waves. I can't let go, I fear.
A weight that I cannot endure without a thousand tears,
and a thousand sweet words still would not make you hear
how deep my love. It's in my bones, my blood, it is soul deep.
Each day, I long for you and now within my heart I keep
you and my love, and each night - alone I softly weep.

54

How can I explain this? But then I wonder, need I?
This love that happened, but never happened too,
I don't see the logic in this situation, reason will belie.
There is no way to understand or discern for you.
I honestly cannot disclose, cannot prove or verify
the miracle that I perceived - too lengthy a review.
The love I knew, was entirely within my heart and eye
yet not just my imagination, there is proof it's true.
If you believe in synchronicity, I cannot deny.
But hard evidence, I fear is long past overdue.
The fact I love you, with everything I am, I sigh!
Still, you ever said a single word but many to construe
this love that happened, real for me. Was it real for you?

55

You... and then words fail me. All I can do
is repeat myself and pause again. It's you
who fills my heart so much it halts my voice.
A whirling void of lost thoughts, I have no choice.
So I try again to say, there is only one for me
but no worries, even though I know you disagree.
I can only mumble. If you don't want to hear
then don't listen, but I need to be upfront and clear.
You... can't say I never told you, or you didn't know
I gave you everything I am. 'Can't say I didn't show
that time and distance have no meaning - not to me.
Because I believe in past lives, still I can't guarantee.
There's no hard evidence for strange things such as this.
No reason you'd believe, those memories bring me bliss.
How can you understand such a far-out fantasy?
When you look, you can only see this human form that's me.
You... can't see my soul, the light within that loves your light.
What to do, but write you poetry deep into the night.

56

My sandcastle on the beach,
I built it safely out of reach
until the tide came rushing in.
Beneath the ocean's roaring din
my castle had to finally yield,
despite the hours I had kneeled.
I built that keep with caring hands,
and in my dream, it could withstand
the sea. I built a home, my heart's ideal,
to house the love I felt... and feel.
I watched the sea sweep it away
and saw my dream drown in the bay.
So, I'll keep that love inside my heart
where the sea cannot wash us apart.

57

Spring's buds and blossoms fade, and now in turn they're gone,
given way to midsummer's heat. The scorching days are long.
How could I think this sweet and idle dream would last
when eight chaotic years sped by entirely too fast?
Longingly, I breathed your name, in the dark each night
and held you in my arms until sunrise and morning light.
I sent you all my love, an extravagant display.
Thousands of poems written, my devotion to convey
my light loves your light. Yet there's only nonchalance,
you stubbornly withhold a single personal response -
or I would not be tempted now, to let you go.
This is infinite eternal love, (not like you don't know).
Like an ocean's high tide, I will recede one day.
It seems that you've decided to let me slowly ebb away.

58

Too far to swim, too many years, too many miles to walk,
no matter what, we cannot seem to find a way to talk.
There isn't any place inside my heart you didn't touch.
No place you don't illuminate, too often and too much;
no crevice, dent or chip, or dark corner that was hidden.
The light washed over me... unexpected and unbidden.
Your heart's another story, it's a citadel to breach.
It's remote and self-protecting, a place I cannot reach.
I don't stand a chance at all, doesn't matter where you are,
to touch inside your heart because I cannot reach that far.

59

I guess it's finally time to leave you, after all these years.
I adored you from afar—I've kept these pearls that are my
tears.
Me, who is immersed in an emotion ocean trance,
should finally say goodbye to this impossible romance.
My prince upon the shore, no longer walks alone.
Is it true that unrequited love turns mermaids into foam?
You no longer come to visit that lonely stretch of beach,
no longer do you keep your heart within my constant reach.
Not that you would have me now, aging that I am.
We are different, your home is not the sea in which I swam.
Let me find a brand new current, where I can gently flow
and ride it out to sea in the next strong undertow.
I never thought when this began, I'd ever say goodbye
but it's just until the next life, where again I will stand by.
So, adieu and sayonara. Stay well, I love you still.
You never realized, I always have and always will.

60 Excerpt from a longer piece

… all the while you are dancing to the rhythm in my heart.
I cannot tell you how profound my love, how deep this goes.
I feel it's been entirely too long we've been apart.
Indeed, what shall I do? My face is not the one you chose.
I wish that we could sing our song together one more time.
I promise I won't grasp, be needy, nor will I postpone.
I'll say again - this lifetime, fates and years have been unkind.
What can I say to change your mind, how can I live alone?
Dancing on a moonlit beach with my pleasure and my pain,
it appears I dance alone, and though dancing far apart...
you remain. I wonder, when will I dance with you again
I wonder, will I ever feel I'm dancing in your heart?

Until you make the unconscious conscious, it will direct your life and you will call it fate. -Carl Jung

61

Time goes by so slowly, yet in the twinkling of an eye
one day you will awaken me...again. My soul's reply
will be a love once more unleashed, a heart that's set afire.
Though fate was hard against me, star-crossed, twisted and awry
I have endured this life without you, but often I ask, why?
When all these years I've tried so hard to quell all my desire.
Why did I awaken, in a life where you could not comply?
I've been waiting in the wings for a love I can't deny,
hoping quite against the odds, understanding to acquire.
Protecting you at every turn, so I could see you shine.
Trying hard to comfort you, wishing you were mine.
I could never turn away in your hour of need.
Beloved, can you hear me as we speak from mind to mind?
Can you feel my fingers on your brow easing that furrowed line?
Can you feel the fire burning, as I stumble in my greed?
My heart does not belong to me, and this love...it is divine.
I'll wait until the end of days, or until the stars align.
If only you will waken then, and let love's wings be freed.

62

It's a peculiar thing, but distinctly wonderful to feel
my heart expanding larger than the room so suddenly.
It fills with bliss and love. It is tender and surreal.
It's gentle, sentimental, I feel it transcendentally.
First an ocean of cascading joy... then comes depths of
longing.

63

For once in my life, in my heart I'm truly home,
yet you continue to ignore my plight both day and night.
Days spent by myself, wandering in my mind.
Nights, in the dark, I'm left sleeping here alone.
It will not matter if I try. or if it's with all my might,
I can't catch a break. You still are not inclined
to love me. So, I must continue on my way,
writing poems and dreaming night and day.

64

I fear the coldness in the depths at which I swim
in the emotion ocean's dark and icy deep.
Yet dive I must, for that's the only path to him
and this love is one I cannot put to sleep.
It is the calling, it keeps me moving forward
even in a silent sea, I hear it night and day.
For years this has transpired, and still moving toward
that gleaming light, I haven't figured out a way
to overcome the sad reality with which I'm faced.
When in the looking glass I see reflected
someone who cannot, next to you, be placed.
Together only in my dreams, but they too are affected.
Not often but sometimes, on this vast ocean's shore,
I sit and idle in the sun, there's one thing on my mind.
I don't know how you doubt, it's only you that I adore.
My starfish wishes, all of them... that my heart won't be
declined.

65

You, the oncoming tide. I am but a receding wave
in awe of your vast power. What I had, I gave.
Because too much time had passed me by,
sadly, you are far beyond my reach.
So I left a kiss for you, waiting on the beach.

66

It happened that one day, as prophetically was said,
I stumbled upon a person; they lit within a fire.
The blaze can't be extinguished, and it has only spread.
That fire is eternal, and the flames are rising higher
because we are connected... by a thin red thread.
It's dismal and discouraging. Truth, nothing less than dire.
there's nothing I can change, but look upon that cord with
dread.
Because I'm not allowed to lavish love on my desire.

67

You can't say I never said goodbye.
It was in every word I whispered through my pain.
Goodbye was present each time I foolishly asked, why?
It was every word in which I said, I love in vain.
Every time I told you that I sit alone and sigh.
Goodbye was suggested when I couldn't easily explain
how I became possessed, a love gone so wildly awry
and how in this predicament, could I remain?
Knowing you cannot love me, I will not deny
that I should take my leave, and further not detain.
I cannot change myself to suit, no matter how I try.
With all the tears I cried, could not hold back or restrain,
goodbye was conveyed with your every no reply.

68

You are here, now is all there is. It's all I have desired,
trying not to worry, or think of things to cause me sorrow.
I've been yours alone since long before this life transpired.
Now within my warm embrace, will you love me tomorrow
when the light of day shows all these years, etched upon my
face?
There is no prepackaged youth that I could buy or borrow
so you would see me lovely, vibrant, slim, and full of grace.
Tonight I am surrendering, to all the powers that be...
I bare my soul and let it shine, imploring it's enough
to touch your soul and feed the fire - between us, you and me.
Though I'm a curiosity and my humor's off the cuff...
If only light of day was kind as moonlight then you'd know
this heart is yours alone, but I'm a diamond in the rough.
I say goodbye tonight for you, and dawn's regrets, forego.

69

Life has dealt some blows of late; overwhelmed, I want to shout.
I'm longing for some solitude on a deserted beach.
Need to sit next to the ocean, and watch the waves roll out
then watch them come again, sifting for seashells within reach.

That moment after sunset, when the fading day meets dusk,
I wish to think and dream of only you, with joy and ease.
But these past days are hellish, it is so hard to adjust.
I want to be among the many people that I please.

Life has dealt some blows of late; I'm just wanting to lay low
but there are things I should accomplish, I'm in need of that.
Some things to ease my mind, then I can get into the flow
and write some poetry for you, but that's not where I'm at.

As twilight passes quickly, twinkling stars come out to shine.
The moon is full, its silver light so bright there's shadows cast.
A shallow fate is haunting me; I cannot call you mine.
Just as I've always known, this love for you, it is my last.

All through the deepest part of night I look toward the sky.
The blows that life has dealt me will not keep me constrained,
but still, I cannot help this wondering and asking why.
Why I love you in the first place - but no one can explain

70

Call it a habit or call it a neural groove.
Either way, the results still look the same,
I'm stuck in love and cannot move.

71

I wouldn't want to capture love; you should be free to fly,
push past boundaries, rise even higher after falling.
My wish always, that your wishes will come true by and by.
Endlessly, I'd stay with you, if you should think of calling.

72

I need you, in a way you might not understand.
All I want from you, is to journey hand in hand.
Don't want to take advantage or use your body up
but I need a place to put this love that overflows my cup.
The heartbreaks happen often, as love tries to escape.
Yet I'll not beg for crumbs, nor will I bow and scrape.
I simply need someone to love. My heart, it's chosen you
to pour it's given grace upon because this heart - it grew.
Too immense to stay inside this mortal being's chest
too infinite and flowing to have taken any rest.
I need you, in a way you might not understand.
Just let me love you from afar, there will be no demand
that you return a bit, not even tiny grains of sand.
My love is like the ocean's edge, an endless stretch of beach
and nothing you could ever do, is out of my love's reach.

73

This end of cycle comes to close. There's the calling of the sea.
I must return to myself now and just take care of me.
I will sleep inside your heart, just as you will sleep in mine
and I guess that we won't meet again, as if by design.
I'll tell you how I loved you all these many long years lost
but will not tell you of the high and dearly precious cost.
It was something that I chose, a time I dared not decline.
To me, you are too exquisite. And too hard to define
is the rare and priceless treasure I cannot win... your love.
"If only," the secret mantra I whisper in place of
the gratitude I felt, submitting self to the divine.
When will there be a time for me? When will these stars align?
This last nine years passed quickly, but they have been the
best.
My tears come into being knowing I have been so blessed.
Too full of love, too filled with joy, my heart begins to shine.
I am obsessed, I do confess, when drinking too much wine.
Went to sleep at two a.m., writing verse for you at five.
What can I do? For this is when I feel the most alive.
Pouring out my heart, it breaks in two. I cannot confine
all the tender care within, all the love I send of mine.
A hundred meadows flowering so sweetly in the sun
and I am unraveled, crumbled, distraught, and I'm undone.

74

We are each other's sun, each thinking we're the moon
reflecting the other's brilliant light. How could it end so soon?
Instead of saying, 'I'll let you go,' I'll say, 'I set you free'.
Because in the end, my love, that sounds happier to me.
I don't want painful memories, I'll keep the warm and
shining.
I cannot bear the thought of spending all of my life pining.
But if you're free, who knows, someday you might come back
to me.
If not, at least you have your happiness and liberty to 'be'.
I wish to hear your laughter, I long to see you smile
and if you leave me here, it's still all been worthwhile.
Instead of saying, 'I'll let you go'... I'll say, 'I set you free'
because in the end, my love, it sounds happier to me.

75

The ghost in the moonlight, I know who you really are.
Time has no meaning, across an ocean not too far.
I loved you in an old life, I'll love you in the next
because I always have. Let's put it in some context.
I don't just love your body, or your gentle face.
I love your soul, your scars, where pain has left its trace.
I'll love you, your essence, the soul that I have seen,
until the death of stars, when old souls reconvene.

76

The one person I call to can't hear me.
The one person I look at can't see me.
The one person I cherish doesn't know me.
The one person I've found, who makes my heart pound,
fires my imagination, fills me with inspiration…
That one man, it's a miracle to me that he could even be.
But I'm glad that I can cast my gaze upon his nights and days.
Without one person to adore, who would I love, like none
before?

77

I will sleep inside your heart, just as you will sleep in mine
You'll become my favorite secret, but then, you've always been…
surrendering to years that pass, await a future sign.
There's not another man on earth, I could get wrapped up in.
Now, daily there's no struggle, no more tears to cry, it seems.
I'll keep my promise. Wish you well, it is for both our sake,
as we continue to rendezvous in our frequent dreams.
Alas! These sweet dreams, so promptly forgotten when we
wake.

I simply remember, I saw you standing there with me.
It is the last part in the dream of ours, I'm reaching out.
You take my hand and smile, there's nothing else that I can see.
But day-to-day reality intrudes and causes doubt.
If loving is a rose, then this great longing is the thorn -
I surrender you again, when I recognize the feel.
This is not a loss to me, it's an interim I've sworn
and abide by, until the future dreaming can be real.

78

I've had as many hopes as grains of sand upon the beach.
How many 'might have beens' sunken to the ocean floor?
It's okay you didn't give me hope, far out past my reach -
too far. But I held tightly to those hopes, and more...
I had dreams that we could reach beyond our mortal forms.
Prayers that we could rise together, as our souls and minds,
to cope with this connection and weather all the storms.
To expand our hearts, because that confounded red thread
binds.
I wish that I was not aware, yet I'm thankful that I am.
But I can't catch a break - luck is elusive, just like you.
Time, a jealous mistress, doesn't give a tinker's damn.
Still, my soul is waiting for the one my love flows to.

79

And if I could, I would
kiss your every scar, each mar
more sweetly than I would discreetly.
Drifting far from shore, hoping - I implore
that I can navigate the deep and learn to keep
from drowning in my own saltwater sea.
The buoy bells are swinging, loudly dinging
they inform, take shelter from the storm!
Yes, even Neptune's daughters know rough waters.
Though endless waves may come and go
it's Luna makes tides ebb and flow.
And this unending love, a boundless ocean
ever deep, it is eternally in motion.
I am caught, and I cannot undo this knot
that keeps me tied, and true to you...
this mermaid I've turned into.

80

I know I wrote the same poem a thousand different days.
No matter how I felt, it seemed a thousand different ways.
Now it occurs to me there's really only three arrays.
Version one was so full of joy that I could fly.
The second, so painful I need to say goodbye
and in the last, I wonder WTF. I'm asking... "Why?"

81 Excerpt from a longer piece

Mermaid tears, they too are pearls,
symbols of the moon that shines
along with starlight sparkling
on the open ocean waves
reminding me I stood by you.
Despite these tears of brine
your heart was more important...
than what this lone mermaid craves.

82

Have you missed me? But I'm still here, I have not gone.
I'm simply standing in the back, and you can't see
that I am going to go to sleep for a while. It won't seem long.
Dreaming in our secret world, I'll love you to the nth degree.
You needn't worry that I've left, because I cannot go.
There is a part of me I gave you all those long years past,
I know it's alive and breathing deeply inside you, so...
the promise is I'll love you, until the very last.
Have you missed me? I'm still here. I've not gone away.
I'm simply standing in the back waiting for a chance.
One day in a future life, when we meet again,
openly for all to see our hearts together in a dance.
But while you live and share this life, I'll stand in back and
wait.
I cannot apologize enough, for this life's twisted fate.

83

It's mystical and marvelous and I know you think it's weird
when, in fact I have to tell you - reality is multi-tiered.
The energy between us cannot be denied at all.
The frequency, it resonates, even though you don't recall
all those lives that went before. Yet time does not exist.
You must think that I'm annoying, because I still persist
in trying to remind you of this red thread connection.
I have never wanted anything but to give of my affection.
You don't need to love me back, I don't require your time,
yet I'd be lying if I said I don't want your heart as mine.
How can I tell you of my love, my undying deep devotion?
How can I keep on telling you it's more boundless than the
ocean?
I've come to think that I've transformed because I overstayed
in the emotion ocean's depths, and I've turned into this
mermaid.
But all this poetry, the love, it seems a useless goal
when you cannot remember, nor can you see my soul.
Alas, upon a lonely beach, I'll just turn into foam
I leave for you a thousand pearls, and my heart within this
tome.

84

If it wasn't destined, why would I sacrifice myself for you?
Or am I? Maybe I'm sacrificing myself for love alone, or
worse—
what if I offer myself, surrendering everything I am because
I thought it was expected and necessary to obtain some
measure
of appreciation? If not love, then perhaps a mere
acknowledgment,
or maybe a spare moment of superficial feigned affection.
If it wasn't destined, why is it you, of all people, and not
someone
who would or could consider me? Why is it you? Why?
If it wasn't destined, how do I account for all the strange and
frequent synchronicities? The connection, all the coincidences
and most of all, what about the overpowering magnet
that pulls my heart right out of my chest and across an ocean.
For what? I get nothing. Actually, I ask for nothing,
but what good would it do if I did ask? That would be
just another disappointment. If it wasn't meant to be,
why does grace shower down on me cascading into bliss
until the body can no longer hold it - just looking at you?
How does this even happen? How can it be?
If it wasn't destined, how do I account for natal charts of stars
and planets aligned to mesmerize me half a world away
and cause the waiting... the wishing I could hold you every
night?
If it wasn't destined, how could you turn me inside out,
and my life upside-down without a word or gesture?
What of these deep soul transformations?
Why are my arms empty and my heart a hollow space until
you smile? Why do I cry when I feel the love flooding in?

If it wasn't destined, why have I spent the better part of
the last decade in utterly devoted adoration, unconditionally
giving of my energy dozens of times a day - every day?
If it wasn't destined, why do I suffer dark nights of the soul,
or this sacred blaze within my heart, this raging holy fire?
If it's not meant to be, why the mingled joy and grief
from which there's no relief? These many years,
why does my soul, remembering, reach out for you?
And someone needs to tell me why...
Why do I feel everything all by myself?

... Ah! I get it now; what I'm supposed to do.
Love myself with all the depth and fierceness.
the tenderness and passion that I felt for you.

85

I've slept a century in moonlight. A tear escapes my eye
as I try to awaken from the dream I've dreamed alone.
How long can I continue sleeping, waiting, on standby
for someone who isn't coming? I try to hold my own.
Had it not been for a shallow fate, that leaves me here to sigh,
had you not been who you are, would my love have once
more grown?
I cannot answer. I can only wish for a reply
as I struggle to revive, even if I am alone.
Either meet me in the dreaming or leave me here to die.
You know I'll rise again someday, your name's etched on my
bones.
There's no such thing as lost and gone, no permanent
goodbye.
You're owner of my heart... but only form becomes outgrown.

86

My spirit spent, near lifeless, felt I had been washed ashore.
This weary form exceeded its far limits long ago.
I gave up on the struggle, I can't do it anymore,
so this is my surrender. I had wanted you to know.
There's no energy within me, I've no reserves in store.
My heart is slowly sinking in the silent depths below
in that emotion ocean, which I talked about before.
I will endure this separation, and stay in the flow -
nothing writes a poem like watching love walk out the door.
Or into someone else's arms... did you really have to go?
Deep within, surrender only means I will explore
the mysteries of yearning, feel the secret longing grow.
Yet I will not disturb your heart, since it's been spoken for.
I'll rest here silently, sleeping within your heart as though
my shining light had dimmed. Some distant day, on some far shore
returning, I will meet you, reignited love bestow.
No longer as a mermaid, and I'll love you... even more.

87

I know I cannot have you, and I thought I was okay
but thinking there's another in your arms I fall apart.
I want you to be happy, so I keep my tears at bay
and I endure it. I will keep you in my tattered heart.
My soul advances toward you, each day in every way.
No end to this feeling, because we never had a start,
still... I don't know how to love you in any other way.

88

Alice through the looking glass
I've left the rabbit hole behind
everything is backward, seems to me.
Life, what is it but dream? Alas!
Often altered space and time.
You must step into it to see.

89

I cannot swallow all these things, words I need to say.
There's too many conversations to leave them all unsaid.
It's enough that I merely speak about my heart to you
so I won't think myself a failure anyway.
My love is constant and even though it remains unfed,
it still grows beyond imagination and into
a waiting ocean, becoming greater by the day.
If only I could focus on that shared dream instead
I'd have the life I'm wishing to pursue.

90

How can I say that I will love you forever?
My dear, forever is not nearly long enough.
This longing song upon my lips, will you sing too?
A soul song sweetly shared; to me, that's proof of love.
What life have I to give you but this present one?
Still I vow, in all lives yet to come, I'm yours.
Whispers in a passing wind have well assured me
you're from a lifetime long ago - centuries past.
I raise a lamp to light the winding path ahead
and there I see attached to me, a long red thread.
I can say I want to stay with you forever
yet if not now, I will wait... wait until whenever.

91

I've only lately thought, I wish I didn't love you
(not the way I do) but the feeling passes in a flash.
Then I remember all the reasons that I do
and the ocean pulls me in - I know I'm going to crash.
Perhaps you think I'm silly, I fell in love too fast
but I'm not falling out. I just get deeper every year.
I never thought ahead, to how long this would last
and never did I think to have some common sense or fear.
If you want to speak of cycles, beginnings and the end,
about the contrasts between hope and despair
recall a previous conversation that I did extend.
Revel and rampage, love and apathy. Love isn't fair.
Just because you offer it, doesn't mean you will receive.
Regardless, give your love so it can flow its blessing.
Simply be prepared, so you won't have to grieve.
Don't have any expectations, or you will be kept guessing.
I've only lately thought, I wish I didn't love you,
but I'm happy to have had the chances that I had
to write this poetry and the courage to pursue
the opportunity to let you drive me mad.

92

This incessant silent longing, I slowly close my eyes
and I imagine - I rest my head upon your sleeve.
The dream flows, the dreamer sleeps, fast the summer flies,
I didn't know that it would hurt this much to leave.
I'll carry on, if you can really call it living.
All day, every day, my heart recalls the past.
If I only had the chance, I would continue giving,
but I guess I knew this love affair wasn't meant to last.
I'm still wishing my dear dream was real and I, belonging.
Then I would not know this incessant, silent longing.

93

Everybody has a secret fear they've hidden or denied
or shoved into mind's basement, buried in the dim and damp.
We each must slay our demons, no matter where they hide.
Whatever darkness dwells within you, let me lift a lamp
and shine it on the shadows, so all your fears subside.
I vowed I'd always love you. I cannot now recant,
I'll defend you from the enemy, the one you keep inside.
My only fear is losing you, so I'm your sword and shield
Just tell me where to find it, I will stare into its eyes -
the battle's just beginning and I will never yield.
I'll never give it power or believe it's taunting lies,
against all false illusion I'll have my courage steeled.
I will sit with them, those shadows, and I will let them cry
until they're small enough to fit my hand. When healed,
I will embrace them, every one, until they're just a sigh.

94

The longing is intense, the yearning more than real.
How can I accept this situation as I am, when...
I cannot be the one for you, this time around?

That first recollection, remembering how I feel.
Not just then, but always and once more, still and again...
I am undone in love now that you've been refound.

Is fate this cruel to hand me a hurtful, faulty deal
wherein I find you, but I do not match? And then
I come apart! Undone in love, unraveled and unwound.

95

...All I have left is the sound of your whisper in my ear
and this great love with its misty memories concealing
a confusing clouded past - and at this point, nothing's clear.
So far inside my heart, layer by layer revealing
I must keep digging deeper, I cannot succumb to fear.

Won't you meet me in Jardin? Because I sorely miss you.
Besides feeling empty, for me there's some things can be
changed.
I'll be your moon, we'll count the stars, the universe in view.
You've always been the sun to me, and though it may sound
strange
My love keeps growing larger, a shared dream overdue.

You had me at hello and here you are at your goodbye.
These years of loving you I'm still unanswered... tell me why?

96

Aware of self as soul, and you a light that dwells within.
You do not know or understand the things that I have seen.
This has been my Waterloo, my heart's breaking point - my
'sin'.
Loving you until the day I die, parting unforeseen.
I'll leave you for a time, so you can better understand
this life's a grand illusion, and not all is as it seems.
My heart is torn as I step back from reaching for your hand.
There aren't any expectations, just wishes, hopes and dreams.

97

I've tried every way I know, to fool myself.
But tonight I had a rather somber thought,
If I love you, I can't store it on a shelf.
If I have it, I should give it. Should I not?

You had me at hello, that first shining smile,
and your eyes reintroduced us long before.
A familiar gaze, heart fluttered for awhile
briefly, yet repeatedly. I could not ignore.

It was then I recalled it's someone just like you
who I'd thought was an ideal, an idle dream.
Looking for you all my life, you're long overdue!
Now what do I do, when our difference is extreme?

98

This cold winter night, in the dark, I'm missing you.
Only a wisp remains from where you previously stood.
A fragment, an impression of a memory, and too,
the phantom image in my mind, its substance not withstood.
In grasping at those hazy wisps, like smoke they disappear,
reaching for my music, I play our favorite song.
Possessed of that sweet melody I soon forget my fear,
vividly I feel the lover to whom my heart belongs.
This cold winter night, by enchanted candlelight I dance;
a solitary form, but there's two shadows on the wall.
Imagining a moonlit beach, my lover's comely glance;
I dream, I dance, and I wait, giving you my endless all.

99

When I'm thinking of you and I want to talk
I'll whisper in the wind and hope the message gets to you.
I'd tell you if I could, but it's too far to walk
just to have you turn around and go the other way.
When I'm missing you, I'll tell it to the river
watch it flow into the ocean, and away.
To carry all my sadness and secretly deliver
it to be immersed and merged with love
that remains an ocean wide and two seas deep.
And if you would accept me, that would be paradise
but since you won't, I cannot, and I dare not keep
this longing to gaze deeply into your eyes.

100

I wish that I could love you lightly, it would ease the pain
of knowing I am not for you, not suited, not a match.
I want to love you freely, nothing lost and nothing gained,
so I won't have to heal my heart when trying to detach.

It felt as though my life washed up bedraggled on a shore,
then found you were a shining pearl concealed within my
heart.
The only way I know to love this pearl... is hard core,
but it's not going anywhere. I know we'll have to part.

You are a strange enchanting jewel, a pearl of great price.
All you need to do is smile, I then forget and I'm enticed.
I need to think again, not live in this fool's paradise
and try to love you lightly... not go skating on thin ice.

101

Why do I always find myself back at the very start?
Fate put this hopeless love on endless loop to test my heart.
But now at least I know why the stars played such dismal
trick.
It seems you keep me going with a carrot on a stick,
I play along. When one door closes, I try other doors.
Yet even then, I hit dead-ends, and this poor heart implores:
have some mercy! A nod in my direction would be kind.
I'm not overtly spurned, but I remain... simply declined.
Still I forge onward, a brave warrior, champion of the heart.
One day I hope to find myself next to you, at the start.

102

Wishing to part your lips with mine, but I cannot.
Hoping for a simple gesture, perhaps a fleeting thought.
But time keeps passing while I wait for love to quit.
Wondering, do I spend time, or merely just endure it?
The clock's tick-tock marks space, between my joy and ache,
a fervent and desirous dream from which I cannot wake.
The more I yearn, the stronger felt, the longer it will take.

103

Because of you, I took a road I would not have taken.
I did something, previously, I thought I could not do.
I have changed in many ways, my former self forsaken.
I felt our souls merge and connect, a first... because of you.
Because my love is infinitely more than words convey,
I cannot speak. So silently, I feel and sink into
that profound emotion ocean; it happens every day.
How can I be so mesmerized, and so in love with you?

Part 4: Dawn Draws Near (after the dnots)

Myths are public dreams, dreams are private myths. -Joseph Campbell

104

(included in Wine and Roses)

Some mornings I'm just so damn thankful
for sunbeams and shadow patterns on the wall,
for the aroma of brewed coffee, fresh flowers,
and the cool bare floor beneath my footfall.
Some mornings I'm glad to be alive, knowing
that I've found the magic and mystery in love
that some will never discover. I feel Grace flowing
in my morning reverie, never ending blue skies.
It's okay that you aren't here, I'll see you tonight.
I'll be there waiting, and until then, those sunbeams
will fill the corners in my heart with golden light.

105

There are times when I think I will indulge
in the flood of love that's ever rushing from behind.
It fills the body - endless overflowing. I must divulge
if this is how I die, death by love, I will not mind.

For when souls touch, our ancient hearts are knowing
perfect joy outweighs the past's grief intertwined.
Our destinies are whispered on the wind so softly blowing
But time moves on, the future's not yet been defined.

Your place here in my heart, a space that can't be claimed -
where from the ancient past, heart's memories remained.
Thus, I write these deep emotions, and the new thereof,
and these pretty songs are painted... with poetry and love.

106

Until the heart stops beating, and I've exhaled my last breath,
until the body has grown cold and confirms my mortal death,
even after. When the lifeless form relinquishes its ghost,
and soul presides, I'll swiftly fly to that far distant coast.
These words of praise and admiration, the passion that I
wrote,
and this love of mine is all I have keeping me afloat.
Until the heart stops beating and I have slowly breathed my
last,
you'll fill all the empty spaces inside my heart of glass.

107

As I sit with my pain, it is in silence.
I allow it as I'm sinking to the bottom of this well.
It is in this dark night, I profoundly contemplate
all of life, of love, and its expense.
Alone, in an ocean of emotion do I dwell.
How long can I survive in this suspended state?
I wrestle with myself, trying to make sense.
When will I see the light? How can I tell?
I go dormant; in my distress I simply feel and wait
until the agony, it starts subsiding,
until the muddy water becomes clear.
It takes a while to transmute this awful state,
you know... my desire and my reality colliding.
I'm working through illusion and my fear,
and I will accept, on my own terms, this fate.
Knowing all the while soul is providing,
and the light within will surely reappear.
It may take a long time, yet I am never late.
I'm sitting with my pain. I sit alone,
until, in the dark, my heart begins to glow.
I do not fear the darkness, I've come to make a friend.
It's teaching me, within is my true home.
Dimly shining, growing brighter, I say hello.
I've survived another shadow, another 'end.'
Unafraid of the chasm, the abyss. The dark's demise
comes with the light - deep inside the grief, I turn it on.
Like a sleeping phoenix I awaken and arise
and the more I light the darkness, the more of it is gone.

108

One light drawn to another, a soul in love with yours.
Yet in that stream of consciousness, without any limitation
I will quietly adore you from where I am, though heart
implores
you meet me in our place to merge in endless celebration.
I write you poetry and send it, hoping it unlocks some doors
you previously closed. I'm in for the duration.
There is a meeting of our minds intended to explore
the universe, the world beyond in playful liberation.
Wherein that world, one stream of consciousness adores
the other stream of light who shares in dual emanation.
What love I have, and can't bestow on you, I keep in store
in hopes that we enjoy more reality creation.

109

I hope you don't think... that this isn't strange for me.
Of course it is, beyond any unexpected blessing.
How can I think that you would or could believe
such nonsense I keep spouting. Yes, I am obsessing.

I freely do confess all my hidden faults and flaws.
Of course I say I'm crazy, make humor like I'm bold
so you never know how serious I am. Then I withdraw
when I am loving you beyond what heart will hold.

I cannot sustain such love without a sign from you.
The burden is too heavy; the love, it is too great
for one alone. It must be shared, so I can hold onto
the wings that make me soar in joy - so I can meet my fate.

Loving you this way, from here, it's hard but I won't quit.
I vacillate and hesitate, so you won't know how deep
love runs. It runs into my bones, yet you will not permit
a space inside your heart. You are not someone I can keep.

I run away at intervals, because I fear you'll know
quite honestly it's you I love, but I cannot discern
that you could ever feel the same. Although...
if wishing made it so, I quickly would return.

110

It wells up from within, affection I cannot hold back
my eyes have feasted on him and there's nothing that I lack
When gaze is fixed on my Beloved, it's no idle whim
that I anticipate and wait for some small word from him.
When the emotion ocean rises, surges, swells, and moves
heart's full, expanding, any forward movement thus removes
all doubt of this connection, then I hunger for his touch.
I didn't know I could delight in someone quite this much.
Four o'clock each afternoon, my sweet reverie ascribed
to visions I receive and I do faithfully transcribe
that swift desirous flush, the exhilarating rush.
I assure you it's enough to make anybody blush.
It wells up from within - this dreadful heart-wrench that I feel
intoxicating, overwhelming, it all seems surreal.
I almost cannot breathe, my gaze fixed only upon him,
his brightly shining light; the sun in heaven seems to dim.

111

I don't need to say I love you, just look into my eyes
all the poetry and love songs, any mortal could devise,
are there within these aqua pools. I've not always been a
mermaid
but swim in the emotion ocean's depths... and I am unafraid.
I'm not scared of your refusal, being shunned, or cast aside.
I never asked you for your love, nor was only lust implied.
You cannot shine, without these moths attracted to your light
especially in the darkest night, that's when you are most
bright.
I don't need to say I love you as I look into your eyes;
it's there I find an infinite and starry paradise.
I'm fine all by myself, and from a distance I adore
just you... won't you accept the love, from this far and distant
shore?

112

Last Sunday of the month, a date I promised to you,
I'd meet you in Jardin for a walk along the beach,
the door between realities, under that flowered tree.
Three years I went there faithfully, love blossomed and it grew.
Jardin is our secret world, it's always within reach.
Close your eyes to see the hilltop next to a turquoise sea.
That world is always waiting; it belongs to you and me.

113

The sun is shining brightly, yet I quiver at your touch.
I am breathless standing still, and I never knew how much
joy a heart could hold. It's overflowing now, so I am bold—
because my heart will burst filled with devotion yet untold.
Still, I stand there in the sunlight, trembling as I look at you
and in this golden light, your eyes that I'm looking deep into
show me the universe, what was the past, what is yet to come.
I see myself reflected and who someday I may become.
Yet I quiver at your touch, even though the day is warm,
and I know absolutely, I'd love you, regardless of your form.
No matter your appearance, no matter where or when.
I am yours, throughout eternity, as I have always been.

114

This kind of love, it is most precious and
the one pearl on the beach, in an endless stretch of sand.
An incomparable, rare and priceless gem,
the most exquisite jewel in my soul's diadem.
So uncommon that I treasure every second,
and you know that I would, if you could only beckon
I'd be with you, regardless of a love that often stings.
But more so do I cherish the pleasure that it brings.
This flame that hotly burns is eternally afire
but it's your light I long for, your heart that I desire.

115

It was no trick of fate, but a well laid plan.
How can I complain when I agreed?
It was another 'level up' as best one can.
Who knew that I would whine and plead
for some acknowledgment, some sign
when giving my whole heart away to you.
Impossible to be with, I cannot make you mine.
This is one tough lesson to get through.

116

Has it gone too far, have I crossed the river
from where I can't return? Can I...
retrace my steps, and take back what was given?
If you won't receive the love, then as the giver
I have lost my cause and I can only cry.
Should I ask of you, that I be forgiven?
How could I dare to thus transgress
and impose upon you to accept my letters?
How should I proceed to take back any love?
Can it be done? No... I cannot repossess
one tiny moment, for there are no debtors,
not in love. What was given is because of...
overwhelming admiration, pure devotion, adoration
and it's offered as redemption for our past.
So very long ago, I cannot easily recall
no matter what time passes, there's no alteration
to this heart, or what it holds. I'm yours until the last.
Even absent, I still find comfort giving you my all.

117

Alas! I did not know I was a mermaid, until you came along.
How could I know, until I met the one soul I'm meant for?
Mermaids can only love but once, no folly, no mistake.
I thought I loved before, but never felt like I belonged
and not once before, did I feel the love down to my core.
Not until you, was it joy or bliss caused my heart to break.
The depths this forces me to swim, to hear your siren song,
your soul, that's calling out to me. How can I love you more?
I can't answer, it's a mystery, more than I can take.
I feel the steady pull as mesmerized I swim along.
Love's growing stronger by the day, a love I can't ignore.
I hold my fierce desire, and yearning... only for your sake.
Because - I didn't know I was a mermaid, until you came
along.

118

I have come all this way for you, just to meet in passing.
Not distance but in lifetimes, our encounters are too brief.
What joy! What anguish, love born from souls forever lasting.
Desire for you, immortal. Time apart, unending grief.
So meet me in our secret place, we'll sit and watch the stars,
we've only minutes plucked from certain hours of the day.
I try my best to cope with this, and healing my old scars
but Darling, won't you meet me? You remain too far away.

119

There is no sorrow, only love; it's comforting to know
that neither time nor distance can leave a hollow space.
No loneliness, and yet the tears still freely flow
but they are tears of joy, in Love's infinite good grace.
I'm always thinking of you. I adore you. Don't you know?
No one can turn my heart aside; you cannot be erased.
There won't be any sad regrets when it's my turn to go.
I hope when I surrender life, I'm deeply gazing on your face
so I can remember clearly, and I am not too slow,
to find you once again and take my rightful place.

120

The problem with a mermaid is she's naive in love
trusting and too honest, a gem set quite above.
So when her prince falls deeply for a human girl,
sadly, our poor mermaid will cry pearl after pearl.
Strung on strings of yearning, this strand reaches far
across the Eastern Sea, at night out to the stars.
Centuries may pass her by, her heart alone steadfast,
for mermaids need a human soul, and true love to last.
When time draws to a close and she must turn to foam
our mermaid sends undying love, to wherever he calls home.

121

What is love? A deep dive inside, into a sublime stillness
that rips holes in your defenses and pretenses because
there's no mindless chatter of the masses to buffer the blows.
You come face to face with your insecurities and self-doubts.
Going deep, old pains and jagged scars that bubbled to the
surface
now and then, swell from an endless sea called the emotion
ocean…
and you better know how to swim.

122

As long as you are who you are, I cannot unlove you,
since I have come to see your light, and understand my soul.
You're more than I dreamed possible, a shining radiant sun,
all the colors in the world. A glorious vibrant hue
flashing through a prism, the rainbows dance out of control -
like my heart, when I hear your voice. In love, I am undone.
Alas I am a mermaid, and about to turn to foam.
I can't ever thoughtlessly, lightly speak love again
for it is everything to me, not something I'll get through.
Your happiness is paramount, there's nothing to atone.
Disappearing in the sea, this great love disperses then
the full measure of the ocean is filled with love for you.
I leave you kisses on the shore. When you walk there alone
…I'll whisper in the sea spray, "It's you who are my home."

123

Years spent sleeping in a cold and darkened cave,
roused by a faint but persistent, distant calling.
She awoke once more, and then began to crave
for that thing, toward which, her soul was slowly crawling.
Weakened from her waiting, the long time that she slept,
this mermaid started swimming for the distant shore.
As she remembered why she went to sleep, she wept.
It was for love, unacknowledged. A love - that was ignored.
Yet sleeping for a century, her love was still alive.
Great Mystery had whispered in her ear a thousand years,
each lifetime spent recalling a love that would revive.
Some lives were spent together, and on parting there were
tears.
Other times in solitude, or a lifetime spent in learning.
But always searching for the one whose soul light brightly
shined
as a beacon in a starless night. The one who caused the
yearning.
The one for whom her own soul had been perfectly designed.

124

You are my sun, my moon and stars, the sky, my universe.
The love I feel so vast, my heart the sea which I traverse.
I have become a mermaid, I know how to swim the deep,
and nothing, no one, ever, will tell me I cannot keep
this treasure I have found. Your siren song, that precious
sound.

You are my guiding star, I'll follow in the black of night.
A diamond sparkling, you're a prism of reflected light.
So many facets, every one an attribute that shines,
so many faces from the past, each one of God's designs.
How perfect you still seem to me, your eyes the master key.

I know you don't remember, it hurts at my heart a bit
but I'll forgive you anything and I'll think little of it.
The universe seems endless, the big picture even more.
It matters not that you forgot, I love you to my core.
My light loves your light, and I will find you - in the darkest
night

125

Cast adrift on the sea of dreams
one cannot believe all that it seems.
The shore too far to try and swim
I close my eyes and I dream of him.
The silver cord observed at night
brings a wishful proxy life to light
but one I cannot dare possess.
Love I only wish I could express.
How grievous this subconscious plot
to remind me all that I have not.
Adrift upon the dreamer's sea
those sweet visions set my bound soul free.
Dreams... become few and far between,
a final ending is yet unseen.
I'll faithfully continue on
but morning comes and the dream is gone.

126

I strain my eyes to see you but cannot stand too near.
Eyes filled with joyful tears—they start to fall.
I cannot look in your direction and not think that I hear
a softly whispered sound, your heart's silent longing call.

I part my lips to speak a cordial soft hello
words of love spill out of them... I have no control.
None of this was planned. But no surprise to me to know
that this abyss is very deep, an unfathomable hole.

I open up my heart, the in-rushing wave too great,
tumbled, I am crushed beneath it but I've learned to swim
like a mermaid, in the depths I need to navigate.
There's not anybody else on earth, that's quite like him.

I breathe it in. Everything I feel and have observed.
Only then, does anything in fact, seem like it's real.
But all this love... disguised. I have to keep it in reserve -
for no one knows the secret that this mermaid must conceal.

127

I have never been more myself than I when I am alone.
Yet I am never truly solitary. With my thoughts...
in our world we have the whole globe to traverse. There's
Tibet,
the Great Wall, Paris glows at night, and golden Tuscany.
I see the emerald isle, alluring Seoul, and Lisbon's tram.
The scent of sea spray on the wind and you are always there.
In my head and in my heart, you are everywhere I am.

128

Hello. I say hello, and say hello once again.
I repeat myself because I cannot say goodbye -
so it's hello. You're always there, underneath my skin.
I cannot get away; it seems I'm always standing by.
I laugh and smile. No one sees how deep the love within.
Sending you good wishes - inside I'm asking why.
Why does it have to be this way? If loving you is wrong - that
is my sin.
Then, I say hello and smile, pretend there's something in my
eye.
But I'm okay! I can get along, and I surely will begin
to make it all sound true. If I could - just learn to say
goodbye.

129

From one world to another, crossing time and space
I anticipate our meetings in our own secluded place.
We make our whispered wishes as stars fall from the sky;
holding hands so tightly, I gaze into your eyes.
We found that place tucked in between sleeping and awake
where there is only truth and love, we blissfully partake
like Peter Pan in Neverland. Believing we can fly... we can!
No boundary, no limits for old souls who have a plan.
The universe spreads overheard, a hundred billion light-years
span.

130

I cannot hold your body, or your light in my embrace
but I can hold you in my heart for an eternity.
It seems I didn't have a chance to be in that sweet place.
I'm out of step in time as well, I'll have to wait and see.
The Sun must keep on shining in its place up in the sky
just because I deeply love, you are not mine own to keep.
I'll hold your heart through dark nights, I'll stop asking why
and while I'm waiting for you, I'll just close my eyes and
sleep.
You are my ever-shining star, the one I cannot lose
so shine your brilliant light, show others how to live
with love and mutual concern, smile and amuse.
Teach people in your own soft way, how to freely give.
I cannot keep you in my dream, perhaps another night...
when the world isn't needing you, when we can be free
to fly the galaxy. "Past the second star, and to the right,
straight on till morning". Beloved, won't you fly with me?

131

I've made a thousand wishes upon stars in the night skies
the only wish come true was to look deeply in your eyes.
Once. I haven't had a second chance to take the pleasure
hidden in your depths, that rare and transcendental treasure.
I know it isn't likely you would find me your desire
but this love burns within, a raging blaze of holy fire.
This path I walk toward you is blessed by every morning sun,
one more day to gaze upon you. A distant race I run
without your acknowledgement, and until the race is done.
No matter if your light loves mine; it remains unspoken.
I cannot cease the doubting, but hope remains unbroken.
You may have thought I said some things you didn't think
were true.
Yet one truth remains - eternal and boundless love for you.
If you were to ask me, I couldn't ever speak a lie
and say I could forsake you. I cannot. In love I die.
I've made a thousand wishes, to be with you at sunrise,
doesn't matter how brief the night. Just looking with your
eyes,
illusion is always there, so... what can you be sure of?
Heart obeys the soul. It's you... always only you, my love.

132

The past spills over the present
when I look into your eyes
and barriers of time and space dissolve.
I find myself transported to another life.
On a windswept hill, the wildflowers in bloom,
you come to me. I know one thing only,
I love you more than my life.
The soul remembers, the heart yearns,
the love lingers. That love has not faded,
not diminished; it lives on because
I promised you it would. I will keep my word.
I will keep you in my heart,
and my soul will always find you.

133

The words fade into the twilight
as feelings overpower them.
No poetry being born... I cannot speak.
Just recollections of a first love -
at least the first one of this kind.
Shy in the beginning, I could not confess,
but the pool of love became an ocean.
The ocean got deeper. The current stronger,
until I am bowled over every time the tide comes in.
Caught up in the undertow as waves break
I am dragged, body and soul, sinking
into this profound love for you.
And then rising, I break the surface
drenched with joy as boundless,
wide and wild as the sea.

*We meet ourselves time and again in a thousand
disguises on the path of life. -Carl Jung*

134 The Hero's Journey

No matter what I say or do, I cannot make you feel.
You've been my awakener to a lifelong holy quest.
After seeking decades past I thought the Grail isn't real.
So many long years seeking, I need comfort and some rest.
Now, looking deep inside myself I find that - there you are!
I'd been looking outside for the one who was within.
I'd been trying to become complete, seeking near and far
when all the while, I contained every answer to begin.

There is no place that I can go alone, you are there too.
Within, but like my shadow, and I found I loved myself
for we are one, every where and when. So precious, loving
you,
my heart has healed. Soul finally determined to live as itself -
live every vibrant moment in communion in the light.
In the understanding 'all is one', there is no need for fears
but I am sentimental and used to dreaming you each night.
I can't express my gratitude, there's no more need of tears.

When moving on without you, I will have to laugh
I can't go anywhere alone, you're still alive inside.
Endings, quite like death - a door to my other half.
Now it's time to water flowers with all the tears I cried.
I'll see you in the after-life or maybe next time round.
No matter what I said, won't you forgive my long ordeal?
I hoped you might recall some of those memories I found
but I will give up driving; it's your turn at the wheel.

135

To be seen for my appearance, common, it is 'the norm'.
But when someone looks beneath, beyond apparent form,
having been discovered, I feel I'm found and I'm undone.
I have been truly seen, my heart starts shining like the sun.
Most people are believing what they see with eyes alone
and fail to find the soul within, which is to most unknown.

It touches deeply in my heart space, because you can't suspect
-
to realize you're recognized has a mysterious effect.
What can I say when you have seen me for who I truly am?
You must know how far I've come, the oceans that I swam
to be here like this now. To know I love... no limitations.
Yet, wishing once again, for long moonlit conversations.

How can I forget you when you've seen me inside out?
How can I explain my heart so you won't have a doubt?
That what I say to you is truly heartfelt and sincere
and I wish that I could whisper, "I love you" in your ear.
To you who has discovered the real me, deep within,
I cannot conceive an ending when I want only to begin.

136

If this love wasn't destined, how does it exist at all?
If I was never meant to love you, why then did I fall?
I have given you my heart, you're connected to my soul
born half a world away, how do I survive at all?
Through all of this confusion and illusion, I can't see …
I've no choice and have to question, just how this can be?
This love buried in my heart, yours in every way.
If this is karma, are these the dues that I must pay?
We will meet again, and someday when you're mine
you will once more remember me from somewhere in time.

137

You are the breath in my whisper, the shimmering horizon at
sunset,
the eye of the storm, the thunderous quiet. You are the
motionless flying arrow,
the peace in the chaos, Divinity in the human heart, tears of
joy.
Paradoxes are present, and they are resolved in the eternal
holy instant
that is now. In this moment, in the sacred dancing stillness of
my love.

138

You keep forgetting, I merely wear a cloak, as Rumi said.
Look for the wearer, the soul inside is who I am, although
the cloak is old, our frequencies are still the same.
Outside of my body, I am brilliant light that shines
just as you're my blazing sun in deepest space.
I'm a shimmering, sparkling energy, a conscious flow
and you're as old as I am. We're both older than stardust,
as ancient as the universe, as sacred as they come.
But it seems you have forgotten and therefore do not know.

139

I exist in two places, here and there.
My heart is with you wherever you are, it seems.
You also lead a double life. There where you are,
and here with me inside my dreams.

140

I know I sound crazy. I used to joke about it.
It's so unbelievable, who could accept?
Yet knowing what I know I need to fit
and unify all the puzzle pieces into one concept.
For most, it's too weird and strange to think legit.
I can tell you all the synchronicities but don't believe
there's such a thing as luck or coincidence at all.
No matter if I wear my heart upon my sleeve,
until you understand my back's against the wall -
until you can perceive your companion and believe,
my energy still lives with you. Perhaps you recall
our first meeting and how strange it really was?
Your hand felt like my own, once and for all,
that out-of-body thrill was all because
my soul decided it was time for a wake-up call.

141

Sunlight streaming in, all I can think of in this hushed, serene
and silent moment, merely a fragment in time, is you.
It makes me smile, content to look upon this lovely scene
in which you stand there, illumined, lucent and somewhat
dazzled too.
How full the heart which holds you, and how sweet the
shining hours
when we were together, with you enfolded in my arms.
It makes me smile. I'm comforted in knowing that the powers
of love can still transfix me. I yield, succumbing to your
charms.
Though from great distance now, time has passed, yet love
remains
and though soul is eternal, this body... cruelly time devours.
They say that love lives on. I swear to this, the soul retains
each precious moment, recalled from some most cherished
hour.
It creates that one eternal moment we will awaken to
when we have crossed the threshold between now and
beyond.
Passing through death's door first, I will be waiting there for
you.
Nothing in this world, not even death, can break our bond.

142

It sounds crazy, yes, I know that.
It's not logical, rational or sensible.
But if there's no such thing as time,
and all realities are in the present moment,
than that distant future that I long for
somehow, somewhere is now.
In dreams, the alternate reality
that future life - I've found that place.

143 Inspiration from a show

She said, "I'd sell my soul to live a life with you."
If she had only known the truth. It's soul who lives
both long and free, and flows in love and grace
between each mortal span that we eventually outgrew.
Souls can dance among stars and eternally soul gives
its radiance and love when two shining lights embrace.
Then heaven smiles and sends us back to be born anew.

144

Last night, as I lay my head upon my pillow
I closed my eyes and smiled at you... "hello."
I held you in my arms as we flew among the stars,
traversed the universe, to constellations near and far.

We talked about our differences and the ways we are the same.
I don't know when I fell for you, but I know there's none to
blame
for the words you whisper in my ear are those things I've
always known;
this love is rare, deep, profound, and Beloved is my own.

Last night, as I lay my head upon my pillow
I closed my eyes and smiled at you... "hello."
The edges of the universe not too far to go
when you're dreaming, and when wishing makes it so.

145

You must understand why I continue to have doubt,
though time and distance haven't put this fire out.
I have no special favor which others don't receive
Beloved, do you expect me to continue to believe?
I'm at a loss. Without a word and no outward sign
I can't tell, in your dreaming, are you really mine?
Unless you show me - I travail with Eros' dart.
Will you let me know at last, you recognize my heart?

146

This weird relationship, it sounds far-fetched to me.
How we are connected, with dreams and thoughts and poetry
I understand, I really do - but others cannot see
the words and thoughts and energy
that flows between us - you and me.
One person writes a poem, the other one responds.
Even if we think it's just our own afterthought
it's not coincidental, that the feelings correspond.
As Muse you are responsible for the poetry begot.
So why care for opinions of those who won't believe?
It's only that I cannot share, and this solitude relieve.
I'm left with dreams and thoughts and poetry... these few,
yet happy this connects us deeply - me and you.

147

A flower petal softly falls, and then one more.
Here comes the autumn and I find I'm fading fast.
One more petal is left clinging—it's my last hope
that I can hold out long enough. I'm waiting for
that final breath of warmth, as summer's last.
When it comes, there is no regret and I can cope
with anything ahead I may not know.
When this last flower petal touches ground
this great love, will then unimpeded flow.
In death, Love's immortality is found.

148 ...of Jardin

Until you smiled
until you cried
until you spoke
until you sighed
until you woke my heart
there was nothing.
This world did not exist.

149

I'm re-reading every letter already mailed to you;
I sent you all the pieces of my poor fragmented heart.
I still can feel your warmth, your fragrance lingers too
but years just keep on passing even though we live apart.
Those pieces that I sent to you, like a river, flow
into a sea of love. There is no end, and there's no start.
Each fragment bears the watermark of longing tears, although
how could I know, this timeless love would consummate my
heart?

I had to give you everything. Surrender all I've got
in order to discover I was made complete once more.
Within your hands again, my heart. More than I ever
thought,
in dreaming we're together with so much more to explore.
The love, beyond enduring, it is infinite in scope,
transcending my imagination, all mind could embrace.
I am left with this thought only, this thing that I call hope...
waking next to you, I reach out - and softly touch your face.

150

Long ago, I promised I would know you first,
and swore that I would love you now as then.
Looking deeply in your eyes as soul energy dispersed,
so I could remember when I saw you once again.

The love's not just inside of me, I am inside of it,
to taste the meaning of this life, the mystery, the song.
Love holds a special secret, divinity... a bit,
if you truly love without conditions all along.

One day you may discover the whisper on your lips
into an eager ear will quickly lead you straight
into my waiting arms. Then you'll finally come to grips
with love's immortality, and our unfinished fate.

151

In giving to you, I receive,
in letting you go, I free myself.
In staying open and vulnerable
I nurture this love, and when I
allow you to depart, I make room
for the love to grow vast enough
to reach you wherever you are.
There is no separation,
just two sets of experience,
two perceptions, two choices.
Fear and separation, or
unity and love.

152

There's no chaser, there's a processor. A soul without self-love.
There's no runner, but an awakener. Eager to rise above
the grief and pain of our duality, we mistakenly have thought
romance and union of the body is the goal. I'm here to tell
you… it is not.

153

It won't matter. Opinion is just that, nothing more.
I won't let 'them' diminish this, to simply pass it off
as some substitute because I was afraid to venture out.
I chose you, not aware of the depths that I would dive,
unaware the heights I could attain, and still come back alive.
Once I glimpsed your soul, there was no turning back
from this awareness, sentient recognition, reuniting.
There's so much more than I expected, I am consistently
amazed anew at you. This love is sweet beyond belief,
but my heart sighs; our times are few and far too brief.
It's poignant, sentimental, superbly transcendental
yet powerful and potent, as enduring as the sea.
Sometimes I am surprised as a wave inundates me
it pulls me so completely into the deep and blissful blue
…that I can barely breathe for loving you.

154

The fault is mine, I have fallen again into despair
but I shall rise with the dawn. And as my mind awakes
to possibilities, potentialities, I become keenly aware
of those old triggers, programs, and the toll it takes.

Instead of acting wounded, I should have clarified my mind
purified my thought before I tripped and fell
How could I think the worst when you've always been so
kind?
I'm well aware it's me, once more; I put myself through hell.

I'm in for the duration, means what life I've left to live
spent learning how to love myself the way that I love you
unconditional, compassionate, protective. I want to give
all the love I have in store, even though my love's taboo.

I must learn to see the truth in every moment, every hour.
That I am not this body, but a brightly shining light
who loves your light, and in that world I have the power
to transform our reality, as I am there with you, all through
the night.

155

To yearn for the essence of your desire,
love's flame blazing, lights the way
to burn away what Love is not.
Brave the heart baptized by fire,
surrender makes the fear allay,
discloses that for which we sought.
To Love Itself we should aspire.
Leave behind the mortal clay...
soul grows from what the heart has taught.

Part 5: Winging It - Return To Flight

Oh God, help me to believe the truth about myself, no matter how beautiful it is. -Marcrina Wiederkehr

The last several poems in this section have been written recently, in 2022. The poems in the three volumes are not arranged in any chronological order. There may be as many as eight or nine years difference from one poem to the next. However, in Part 5 I wish to express a rising of the spirit from the depths of the emotion ocean. There is resolution, hope, comfort. This is the part of the hero's journey where you slay your beast and start home.

There comes a time when you realize that the Beloved is not the source, but is a facilitator, an Awakener to all the love and joy that we can have, once we accept that is who we are. Beloved was the key to the door of my soul. If that door was locked at any point, it takes a key. For some, this is a soul-connected person. For if not you, who else would have the key but your counterpart? Our counterpart is on their journey to discover the same. Yes, there is resonance. That's for another book.

We are the love we seek. Our Divine Lover is ourselves, there is an inner union of the Anima and Animus, a wholeness of the sacred spirit we are. We are souls, that God-spark essence, the divine part of us which is immortal and eternal. God is indeed Love, the Universe, Source, All That Is. Vocabulary doesn't matter.

The universe doesn't speak English It speaks frequency. -Nassim Haramein

By releasing the past, you let go of all your old boundaries and limitations. Don't you know? You can fly!

157

This 9-year cycle ends and I hear the calling of the sea -
I must be getting to it and just take care of me.
I sink down in the dark. The inner fire starts to burn.
Into the air in flight; belonging there, I must return,
no longer as a mermaid, but a soaring phoenix queen.
No longer am I grieving, it's my time to be seen.

158

Sitting calmly on the beach, peacefully watching the tide roll
in.
There it is, an ocean unfathomably deep, with the power
to sink a fleet of sailing ships, never to be seen again.
I sent my heart across the sea to you, en route it was devoured
swallowed up entirely by the love that it drowned in...
then washed upon your foreign shore in early morning hours.
Slowly, while you were sleeping, I found my way into your
dream.
My heart will survive, will revive, and bloom like wildflowers.
You welcomed me with open arms, heart was at once
redeemed
and love was glorified in souls and the empathy that's ours.

159

Comforting, I am not feeling out in the dark and cold,
and how could I be lonely with my own companion here?
That energetic transfer that happened when we met
maybe you've discovered yours, it's like I'm always near.
Thinking things that you have thought, feelings you have felt.
We share our inspiration, ideas when we write.
The dream life I've experienced would make any woman melt
and explains we must commune in the middle of the night.

160

When I was weakest, you were my strongest motivation
and my heart will follow you, it's no frivolous fixation.
When I felt my saddest, you gave a happy radiant smile
I truly love you, always will. I'll go the extra mile.
When life seemed at its coldest, it was you who kept me
burning.
My heart's on fire daily. I pen poems of my yearning.
When the sun shines in the morning and light gets in your
eyes
I love nothing more than watching you... awaken and arise.

161

Sometimes I think I'm trapped inside an aging body,
one you could not love; it's flawed, used up and shoddy.
So I am urged to move beyond the form and finally realize
I am not this body! Not what's reflected in their eyes,
but a vibrant flowing frequency, a brilliant dancing energy.
Soul to soul, not form to form, all I have to do is trust.
You're as ancient as I am, and we are older than stardust.

162

Waking up this morning, as always. you were on my mind.
I won't be imploring you to take pity or be kind.
I have tied my dreams to love, now I'm going to be me.
I'd never known a love who gave me wings and set me free.
I'll take off on my own and fly, no one can keep me down.
My happiness, the choice is mine, my turn has come around.

Old dreams already came true, new dreams won't depend on you
I'll keep them in my heart, and no one will ever break apart
my dreams and wishes - as many as the sea has fishes.

Waking up this morning, as always, you were on my mind.
This life is mine, it's up to me to choose to redefine.
I won't give up, I won't give in. time and time again
I will achieve my dreams and I decide just when I win.
Though I may seem slow to start, and I've made my own mistakes,
the road's been long and hard, but I've got everything it takes.

Old dreams already came true, new dreams don't depend on you
I keep them in my heart and no one can ever break apart
my dreams and wishes - as many as the sea has fishes.

Waking up this morning, you are forever on my mind.
I have tied my dreams to love, no control and flying blind.
Though merely as a friend I have to thank you in the end,
no matter what the damage done, it seems I always mend.
I can accomplish what I want, in time, in my own way
I'll rise again, and I'll live on to dream another day.

My last dream already true. No fantasy that I outgrew,
Now you know, among your blessings there is me.

163

Your eyes shine in the moonlight, the embers in the fire glow.
Eastern ocean breeze feels cool, yet this love is running hot
as I wrap my thoughts around you. I wish that you could know,
tonight, I will be waiting for you in our secret spot.
And then Beloved, for your exultation I'll bestow
a lavish banquet of delights with everything I've got.
Anything you ask of me, you know I cannot refuse
when the taste of you, one kiss, is about to break my mind.
So imagine anything at all, you need only choose
and that pleasure will be yours as we lie intertwined.
You are my inspiration, my Beloved and my Muse.
I wake and have to leave this precious state of flow behind.

164

You are the sun, I am the moon simply reflecting light.
My face always turned toward you, like a sunflower in a field
among a million other flowers, keeps my identity concealed.
In my emotion ocean, I navigate the depths; tides rise and fall.
Depending on your smile, a glance or even one small frown
my heart can leap, take flight or it can sink and drown.
We spin through space, each set in our own course, we never touch.
Though you, blazing, light the day - I reflect a softer light. I shine
for you each night. It's then Beloved's met and he is mine.

165

This is happiness, lying on my back staring into an azure sky.
It's what I feel when I'm with you. It's called a natural high.
But what good is this, when it's you I miss, and you are not around
to give me that old rush? So I keep my feet upon the ground.
Damn. If only I could lie with you upon that hilltop green,
and talk of things with meaning, and sights we've never seen.
If only I could hold you and say, "I'll love you always.
Whether you are here or there" until the ending of my days.

166

No matter if the sun shone brightly, or the moon was dim,
eventually I'd recognize and surely know it's him.
All I have to do from one earthly life until the next
is follow my heart's call, surviving painful wounds' effects.
As long as I stay resolute, faithful to my heart's home
I'll seek him in wild places, and not the pleasure dome.
I'll cross the desert, and explore the caves and canyons deep
climb the mountain, swim an ocean, my other half to keep.
In a hundred different worlds, only one enchanted wood
and hilltop overlooking, where together we once stood.
That island with the empty beach, perhaps you're waiting there -
seeking me; when found, I'll be shining, radiant and fair.

167

I used to think I missed you, I had longed to hold you tight.
We used to live a life together in my dreams each night,
but for the longest time I didn't know, you're always here -
until the thought occurred to me, you never are not near.
Remembering our meeting, the transfer of energy,
part of me assigned to you, part of you stayed here with me.
Now you can keep me company, though miles and miles
away.
There is no more longing, we walk together every day.
I ponder though, if you've discovered that I walk with you
everywhere you go. I wonder... if you have felt it too.
This wondrous marvel, I can be both here and where you are
no need to travel distance, or for wishing on a star.

168

How many times have I buried my longing?
I cannot count them.
How often has yearning been my only companion?
I have forgotten.
Why has it been you, and only you, these years?
I can't explain… except to say it's a mandate from my soul.
How many times alone, have I searched the stars?
Too many, wishing you were here.
How often did I close my eyes and feel your warmth?
Countless times, precious memories.
Now comes the night and... if I can do this right
my heart and yours together rise in flight.

169

It was heaven, standing by your side, looking up at you
at our dinner party as we entertained our guests.
It felt so right, so comforting, and so commonplace.
Every time that I came near you, reaching out, I drew
my fingertips along your arm, knowing I've been blessed.
You see, my love, our times are few, but they are full of grace.
I've been given moments, precious memories of you
and you brought your pillows to my bed that will attest
you will be returning, though there's not another trace.
It must have been a shared dream, your way to get me
through
because I awoke without you, yet I'm happy, I confess,
that you would come and reassure me that I still have a place.
Those yellow flowers were forsythia that profusely grew,
they mean anticipation, devoted love. At your request
I gathered buds so they could bloom, and wait for your
embrace.

170

Now I've become a mermaid. resting on the ocean floor
I know, in this emotion ocean, I could not become more.
This metamorphosis, it is soul's own evolution,
it's another lesson learned. Seems I'm my own solution.
I was a phoenix after all, and capable of flight.
Rising from the ashes, eternal love again ignites.
It blazes through my body, it's a roaring whirling wind.
My love was grace and beauty, no dishonorable sin.
It was freely given, my love a sacred holy rite
that I surrendered to you as a sacrament each night.
So rest your weary head and heart. The dreaming sets you free.
For now, night flight is still the only way to be with me.
This mermaid will change back, and brightly feathered, take
to air
We'll meet in the Great Mystery, with a poem and a prayer.

171

You helped me achieve a dream I never knew I had.
I thought it was a fantasy, a mere silly idle whim.
Though most of my art, these poems, sound so very sad
what beauty, and what wonder I hold the world and you in.
Beneath your sway I had to write it - so I could express
the sacred essence of this love, it could never be a sin.
It's pure and sacramental, with reverence… noblesse.
Every single 'I love you', is uttered like a hymn.
I pour soul's essence into it with the power I possess
so you can truly feel it, this holy blaze that will not dim.
My love must be eternal, I only wish your happiness.
I've turned into a mermaid, and now it's sink or swim
but I set you free, for me, lest you assume that I obsess.

172

I don't hold a 'little' light, nor am I reflecting yours,
nor am I possessing a blazing holy fire... it is myself.
Pure and sacramental, a firestorm of love that roars,
and gentle glow that warms a heart left sitting on a shelf.
The infinite eternal flame, undying love, is ME.
I am the sacred essence of it, and divinity...
I cannot give you something from within me, I am not.
The key that opens up the gate, the muse who set me free,
he's not the source of all the love, and though it's burning hot,
it was already there. The key simply unlatched the door -
I don't just feel eternal love... it's who I AM, my inner core.

173

When it comes to you, I've no defense, knowing I can't fight
against the karma in this life - and then I see you shine.
As long as you are happy, I cannot complain of slight.
But how could I have guessed, this time with you would
redefine
what it means to love, how long it lasts... that heart would
reignite.
Jardin awaits, come when you can, I'm not a clinging vine.
Nothing matters anymore, but everything will be alright.
We still meet beyond the blue in dreams past the horizon line.

174

My love grows all around you, though unseen.
It's in every flower and tree that you can see.
In every sprouting seed, when light and life convene
love simply grows. Devotion flows to you from me.
The process, never ending, in love's eternal course
though it may be winter now, the spring returns.
In the thriving of this garden, there is no remorse.
My love is constant, undying; it only seemingly adjourns.

175

I just glanced at you and there it was
the starlight in your eyes,
the sunlight in your smile.
You cause me waves of love that send me
on rockets of desire to the moon
and beyond, to distant galaxies and back.
How can I explain what makes my heart
follow where you lead for all these years, except -
it is your light. It shines so bright within.
I see and feel the radiance, the shimmer of your soul
and I cannot, nor will I choose to, forget and let it go.
The universe, our playground,
our dreaming world, another home.
These memories are seared into my mind,
and Mind tells Heart and Soul,
"There's only one who resonates with us
and we'll recognize him anywhere because
we'll see starlight in his eyes, sunlight in his smile
and our light, unerringly, will gravitate to his."

176 Our companions

There are people, when they meet me, who can see two faces.
Not just mine but yours. You are on my left and just behind.
For you exist, not just where you are, but in two places,
and everywhere you are, so is a part of me assigned.
There is no place that I can ever go where you are not
for when I touched you, met your eye, energy cascaded.
At our first meeting, I went out-of-body on the spot -
these companions that we share are the energy we traded.
Sometimes, when I awake, I have been given several lines.
How rare this strange, mystifying, and odd 'companion thing'
when we both receive the same ideas. Perhaps it is a sign
we're connected, heart to heart, mind to mind by this red
string.
How unfortunate that we don't match, yet we're still together
for it's only our appearances that people judge and see.
They don't understand we've known each other since forever
and how can they know we match in frequency?

177

I can gaze deeply in your eyes, as always, I get lost.
But I don't mind at all, to bear the burden of this cost,
I close my eyes and there you are, smelling of raindrops.
My heart fills to the point I think it's going to stop...
so deep in love, even from afar.

My heart's on fire, it blazes for you through the night and day
it calls your name, and quickly answers to your sway.
I can only love you more each day... and more once I die.
Then there is no ego, no incessant wondering why
I had to love you from afar.

I'm not going anywhere - the whole universe is home.
We are all connected, so I never am alone.
Even though I know it, I'm reminded there's no bounds,
no limits to the love. It's always present and surrounds
every heart enduring a loving from afar
...because the love will reach to everywhere you are.

178

I've held you nightly while you sleep
and gazed upon your resting face,
and deftly on my memory
your every feature I have traced.

What kind of heaven can this be
to see you sleeping every dawn?
Your silent form here next to me,
I see you wake and watch you yawn.

I hold you daily in my heart.
I hold you nights in my embrace.
For every moment we're apart,
I hold for you, a sacred space.

179

That safe haven in our dream world brings me so much comfort
I may not remember every time, but when I awake
I know we've been together. Yet my memory's falling short
as I rise and ready for the day. There is no mistake
when my heart reminds me, we are each other's soul consort
beyond the blue, in Jardin's lush and divine paradise.
It merely takes a dream or focused thought and we transport
to Jardin's golden beaches, where both hearts and souls arise.
The tree up on the hilltop, grassy fields in which we lie.
The sky - both sun and moon, witness our splendor in the grass.
When it's time one day, with you ever on my mind, I'll die
and I'll be waiting in Jardin for whom none can surpass.
Soul-piercing. Ah! This love a revelation from on high
If God is Love then I have found my calling. It is true...
I cannot speak for you at all. But I cannot deny
my fate in this reality, it was my Waterloo
but I'm rising from the ashes and now I'm going to fly.

180

I can live quite well without you. You're alive and well inside
this brimming heart. Day and night, your energy is next to
me.
Just behind and on the left so I'm no longer feeling lonely.
The grief and heartache turned to joy and everything sublime.

I've moved beyond the emptiness and all the tears I cried,
to live with you each night, when our souls at play, fly free.
My love, you leave me breathless - enjoy the merging slowly.
Do not rush this part of dreaming, there's no such thing as
time.

Let's go dancing through the universe together, starry-eyed.
We swam in the emotion ocean, now we'll sail the galaxy.
Beloved, never doubt this; you're eternally my only.
When we are out of body, I'm yours, and happily you're mine.

181

What of time? I suspect that we don't understand
how it works or that it's not a spatial attribute
but a series of still moments side by side.
It feels like it flows, but that cannot withstand
the scrutiny, for science too astute.
But darling, time cannot camouflage or hide
this love, experienced firsthand.
It's something that I know deep in my soul
and I am positive, it's nothing I control.

182

All those conversations in your head... imagination or
telepathy?

Gazing at the starry sky, I feel you next to me.
Your phantom form feels soft and warm,
though your image I can't see.
We talk of common things - how was your day?
Yet, how can this be the norm?
How can anyone believe in any way?
A part of me lives there with you
and part of you lives here as well.
Thus, my feral heart is docile and subdued.
When flagrantly I indulge in bliss
it only takes a second for my heart to swell
at the thought of tasting you and your honeyed kiss.
My darling, can you finally, truly understand
this energy accord that is our sacred bond,
this red thread, that keeps me coming on demand?
I never planned this! Seemed fate had gone awry
yet it offers frequent rendezvous in the blue beyond
because the 3D world only leaves me high and dry.

183

You really can't imagine how full my heart
or how happy you have made me on my birthday
I can't imagine being any farther than we are apart,
but distance, it means absolutely nothing anyway
Dreams overcome the distance, there's no such thing as time.
When two hearts are counting stars beneath the moon
or chasing in the sunlight, or together writing rhyme,
a thought can bring you next to me. And now is not too soon
because even though I have withdrawn and I've said goodbye
that only means when we're awake. Silent wishes will redeem
the life we live in poetry, in the twinkling of an eye.
We have forever... to play among the stars and dream.

There can be no transforming of darkness into light and of apathy into movement without emotion. -Carl Jung

184

Your life ends differently than mine, the difference so vast,
at least the fate in this life, but it's not the first nor last.
There'll be many other chapters in our Akashic book,
this episode is temporary, not to be mistook
for any final ending. We can author our own lines
and write a proper romance when we meet next time.
With all the grief and longing, I got caught up in this role -
thought every 3D thing was real, it really took a toll.
Oh, my poor heart, who had been yearning in the wings.
All this painful fuss and bother about red entangled strings.
I've grown a lot, expanded, took the dive into the deep
and when I hit the bottom, I grew wings I'm going to keep.
Don't worry anymore. The focus wasn't only you.
I had to learn to fly again, I need desire to push me through.
Ascending on a silent wind, I soar above the earth,
I've finally realized my own incomparable worth.
In our last separate days, we'll meet far-distant different ends
but I'll wait for you in Jardin. Come claim me then.

185

I no longer yearn to hold you close, I have taken you within.
No longer two but one, an inner union's taken place.
It's all energy, it's soul to soul - not skin to skin.
A cosmic god should understand, we don't require face to face.
It's a crazy situation, or perhaps you think it's me,
but this Mermaid's Tears collection, the last you'll see my verse.
I'm not sharing anymore, no need to tell... when you can see
your own companion if you try. It's truly not a curse.

It's a miracle, in fact. Though it took me a long time
to find out how to deal with it, to learn to integrate.
Despite Wine and Roses, there's seas to swim and mounts to climb.
One day you'll learn to master this Peach Blossom, Red Thread fate.
I never do get lonely; you are here, so why would I?
There's been joyous revelations, glimpses into the Divine.
No longer do I need you to confirm or to deny.
It's all a cosmic sacred plan, all we need do is shine.

186

You cannot see how I look at you, the expression on my face.
They say that when I see you, something within me starts to glow
and I light up from the inside. Overflowing with such grace,
each witness cannot miss the gift that this love has bestowed.
Such radiance, and in this light, because it comes from love,
I bask in warmth and joy, knowing I can never erase
your name... it's etched upon my heart. The tenderness thereof
will never dissipate and all affection that I have for you, I embrace.
You need not love me in return; I have the gifts love brings.
Thus, profoundly I will love you, more with each passing year.
Season after season, my heart has nurtured stronger wings
and all the love I give you, please know, it has always been sincere.

187

Thank you for waking up my heart - for causing love to flow
a mighty river without end. Back then, how could I know
it would be forever love? A timeless gift that would bestow
joy to the heart, and compel my eternal soul to grow.

188

I understand, I truly do, and all is well with me
if everything's okay with you, then there is no regret.
I wanted all the best for you; I'm hoping you can see
that I will always love you, and I never could forget.
You are my greatest love in life, you're the eternal one.
But this is merely one timeline, and I'm with you in dreams.
I truly meant it when I said, you are my brilliant sun,
our two lights shining brightly, merging in one conscious
stream.
Everything's forgiven, it's now time for letting go.
For every timeline that there is, know all of them are now.
There is no loss, no separation, we need only to grow
how much love we offer, and how much love we can allow.

189

Though the night is dark and cool, the stars are shining
brightly.
Thoughts of you, like passing clouds, are reminding me I miss
those days gone by, so long ago, when we embraced so tightly.
I wonder where you've gone. Too fondly, I reminisce
and if you returned, I ponder, would conversation be polite?
Or would that old fire flare, and heat be tasted in a kiss?
Can I entertain such thoughts if I hold them lightly?
But reminiscing brings back feelings, not just the pain, but
bliss.
Good night moon and stars. Do I miss him? I do... slightly.
But I learned to say goodbye and climbed out of the abyss.

190

I'm a phoenix rising from the ashes of my own demise.
A mermaid, in the emotion ocean's depths, ever changing.
I am the scent of spring reborn, fresh winged dragonflies.
The forest and the desert sands shifting, rearranging.
I'm the mystery of night; stars burn, emanating light.
I am the Soul who loves you… and there is no wrong or right.

191

I am the melting snow, the wind that has already blown,
the sun that set, and the great loves I'd once known -
but are no longer. Without you, how could I be any more?
The lonesome dove forgetting how to soar,
I am the emptied heart, torn wide open from its longing,
and bruised from my many failed attempts at belonging.
Love poured out in your direction, has since washed back
ashore.
I'm realizing now, I'm who I've been waiting for.

Your visions will become clear only when you can look into your own heart. Who looks outside, dreams; who looks inside, awakes. -Carl Jung

Part 6: The Hero's Return

> *The meeting of two personalities is like the contact of two chemical substances: if there is any reaction, both are transformed. -Carl Jung*

I'll bring this around to the ending of the hero's journey and tie up some loose ends. My last challenges were making the decision to share these poems, thoughts, and emotions. Would I be brave enough to publish despite other people's opinions? I made the decision, started selecting them, found an editor and I set myself a deadline. I published Peach Blossoms and Red Threads and felt somewhat exposed, but nothing bad happened. The second book was braver; I included more poems. I didn't do this for anyone other than myself. Muse has already seen 90% of them.

In this volume, pearls are the tears our Mermaid weeps. They are things of beauty and great value. Tears are a blessing. Look what we go through to get them. They offer us a release, helping those emotions flow instead of getting stuck.

> *There is a sacredness in tears. They are not the mark of weakness, but of power. They speak more eloquently than ten thousand tongues. They are messengers of overwhelming grief... and unspeakable love. -Washington Irving*

Tears are witness to shame, humiliation, and tremendous pain. But they also express immeasurable beauty and appreciation, gratitude, deep compassion and joy when you are so overcome you cannot speak words. Simply gazing at Muse for a few seconds too long, I would weep. I couldn't tell you why, I often wondered. But the tears came without warning and without resistance. With an easy flow, tears visited almost daily for years. I was not ashamed to entertain them. I felt there was a purpose for them, as if they were washing away some old grief with an overwhelming gratitude. I forgave, and asked to be forgiven for whatever I was grieving.

When I hear "a mermaid's tears," I think of pearls of wisdom. When we gain wisdom, we often pay for a hard lesson with our tears. At the end of this volume, it's only fitting to complete the hero's quest. Returning with the prize, the treasure which was won. That pearl of great price...

I have bared my soul here. Every poem lamenting my situation was a struggle to make sense of things that wouldn't normally make sense and for which there is no evidence. It was a fight against futility and loss of hope. Every bit of bliss was joy beyond anything I'd known, also without making sense to any onlooker. The battle to believe and trust my own knowing despite the fact I couldn't guarantee it, was a thousand-mile journey. There was always a little nagging doubt, a step backward to haunt me after every two steps forward. One step, one slow step at a time, made for a long trip. Still, I like to think everything happens for a reason. I also like to think the universe is a benevolent place, God is Love and Love conquers all.

Before closing the last chapter of this last volume of poems, I decided I would add some very special poems. These have a deep place in my heart. They may not seem significant to anyone else, but I hold them very dear. They are dated and in chronological order. I have made a decision this will be the last book of poems, though probably not the last book.

I have one challenge yet to meet. That is to get this last volume delivered.

Namaste, my friend; I wish you the best and brightest. I wish you every happiness and lots of journeys.

September 5, 2022

192 March 10, 2015

"FOG" - Something that obscures or conceals; a haze. A state
of mental vagueness or bewilderment (or both)

I can't help myself, I trip over the threshold.
Stumbling into a fog in which I can see only you,
right in front of me. Everything else is obscured,
dim and muted in the silence of my stilled mind.
I can feel my heart pound as it pulses love through my veins.
The heart that beats for you; blood so hot I am on fire.
There in the fog, you and me, and my desire.

193 February 14, 2018

"One Song"

I have one song that is my own,
it is the song my heart sings.
I've only one, it plays alone.
It begins when your smile brings
me to the edge of paradise,
and your gaze, to Eden's gates -
a place no mortal could devise.
I'll sing on despite our fates,
our fears, the burdens that we bear.
I'll send my soul song straight to you,
whispered like prayer
and hope... that you already knew.

194 March 7, 2018

This wasn't a poem, it was a letter I wrote. I've decided to arrange it a little bit and see how that works. I was explaining about dragonfly and sending that energy. I said, among other things, "Change is in the wind. You can do it, and you will fly bright and happy in the sunlight, free of the past. Courageous and Victorious. Don't back down, no retreat, fly forward and overcome this challenge. Dragonfly has many positive meanings. It is a symbol for the samurai that represents to never give up."

Change is in the wind. Though you may not believe,
I care and I will help you in any way I can.
Don't be afraid because you were deceived.
Don't let anyone, or how they hurt you,
take your life or dream away.
You are not alone, you're loved. I'll hold your hand.
You will fly freely in the sun, bask in the light of day
and overcome this challenge. The past - just let it go.
Don't carry your mistakes around;
rise up and overcome your limits.
Fly forward; no retreat, and don't back down.
Your soul cannot be dimmed by pain
so never give it up. You're my sun, a dazzling light,
and souls shine pure forever. Don't lose your dream.
Don't let them win. Have courage to rise up in flight.
I'll walk through hell with you, together.

195 March 7, 2018

A retro sort of poem. An answer, to an answer, to a letter.
This cannot be considered an entirely original poem for that
reason, though several lines and line fragments have appeared
in my earlier writing.

No matter what we understand,
I cannot touch you from where I am.
Just close your eyes and whisper in my ear.
Your arms too far, the dream unclear.
I want you to hold me close to your heart.
Every day, I ask for a love like you to start
a shared dream, and I will not care
if you are not mine, because I cannot be there.
But in that dream I wish I'd never wake.
I can feel your breath; I sigh from one more heartbreak.
Close your eyes, hold me in your arms so I can't leave.
If you tell me I am beautiful, I will believe.
I'll hold your hand, so stay with me tonight.
Don't abandon me, you are my one delight.
I don't want to wake from dreams in which I hold you.
This misery is also joy, and it's going to get me through.

196 May 20, 2019

I woke up with the first 5 lines of this poem already in my
head.

Every single morning, my very first thought is of you.
I allow myself the time, give my dreams a quick review.
I want you to hold me close to your heart again tonight,
not minding if these images arouse me or excite.
You are my dazzling sun, my deepest joy, my greatest pain.
Your smile, always shining brightly, pure and unprofaned.
Dream lover, I'm not sure what else there is that I can do,
except explain this paradise created just for you.
There truly is a safer place for heart to call a home,
so just let me love you, and you won't need to dream alone.
Can you accept my love, whose core reality ignores
the far boundaries of what we know? For it dares explore
the further limits of the soul, the shores of heart and mind,
the edges of the universe. And so far, what I find...
is this, each and every morning my first thought is of you.
A dreaming love relationship, I've clearly thought it through.
While sleeping, we can lead a double life. A slower pace
to hide from prying, public eyes and bask in love's embrace.
A secret rendezvous, whispered sweet nothings in my ear.
In lucid dreams there is no one and nothing left to fear.
So I'll be waiting in that place, expecting you tonight.
I'll meet you on that hilltop, for an afternoon's delight.
Dream lover, close your eyes and wish, then all you have to do
is show up, and I'll give my tender, doting heart to you.

197 August 27, 2019

If not from dreams, I don't know where it comes from
unless it's shared thoughts. Telepathy or "spooky action at a
distance"?

If I'm feeling down, if I'm adrift and all alone
I can turn and you are there to comfort me.
Some part of you has never left my side
nor has that part of me ever left from you.
I am in awe, and entirely enthralled
that such things as these exist and cannot hide.
If I take too long to gaze into your eyes,
the universe unfolds, and I AM Love.
Embracing all the nations, all that swims and flies
Love for everything, below, beside, above.
Because you are next to me, not in form
but in your essence. It is your spirit
holds me close and keeps me warm.
Sing that whispering song, and I will hear it.

198 February 11, 2019

Remember when I wrote to you, the night that I drank wine?
I said I'd found the courage to say things on my mind.
I'm glad you read that letter; it was written to inform.
Now you positively know, you took my heart by storm.
I can't explain these circumstances - why this is! Alas,
but it's you who caused the smile in the bottom of my glass.
You alone can shake my world, and if you understand,
beyond the endless blue, we'll meet as previously planned

199 March 22, 2020

My dark-eyed darling, the whole wide world is in your eyes.
When I look deep I see it all. I find everything I need
and more... I see the people striving, trying to survive
I feel their loneliness and aching, I feel it when they bleed.
But through the tears I shed, here with you, I find
the strength in conquering all fears. Love will beat its drum.
Together we can see this to the end by being kind.
I see it in your eyes, I know that love will overcome.

200 May 1, 2020

I remember sadly now, how it was, two summers back,
that dark night of the soul, that cruel affliction was for me.
Plunged deep in the abyss, because of everything I lack,
knowing you are too far for me. On that all can agree.
I wept into the deepest hours of every night, and then
spent hellish hours sobbing in my pillow before dawn
aware I'd spent the whole night, longing for you - once again.
Wishing you were closer, to rest my weary head upon.
It seemed I was anemic, all night I was bleeding love.
Yet I couldn't stop the sorrow, each sigh I thought my last.
I'm thankful that it was a phase, something I grew out of.
I survived those months, and those melancholy days slid past.

About the Author

Linda Harris is a poet and writer. This is her third book, with more books to come. Having been a writer of custom wedding ceremonies as well as officiant of those weddings, she comes with an appreciation for romance and commitment. Linda served as a spiritual group leader for twenty years, so she's also in touch with the soul of things. Bridging two worlds is nothing new. As a Wisdom teacher and Mystic, Linda enjoys her exploration of astrology, self-healing, higher consciousness, and quantum mechanics. She lives in the Midwest with Joey, her tabby cat, but longs to live near the ocean to pacify her inner mermaid. Linda says she's not a hopeless romantic; rather, a hopeful one.

Also by Linda Harris:

Peach Blossoms and Red Threads
Wine and Roses

www.ingramcontent.com/pod-product-compliance
Lightning Source LLC
Chambersburg PA
CBHW022134150726
47992CB00002B/587